Using Children's Literature to Enhance Reading Instruction

by
Eve Hayes
and DeLinda Youngblood

Carson-Dellosa Publishing Company, Inc.
Greensboro, North Carolina

Credits

Editor

Joey Bland

Cover Design

Annette Hollister-Papp

Cover Illustration

Lisa Olsen

Layout Design

Van Harris

Inside Illustrations

Stefano Giorgi

Dedication

This book is dedicated to Jessica. Thank you for making my life so wonderful!

Eve Hayes

I would like to dedicate this book to six very special people in my life: Randa, who is not only my daughter, but my very best friend; Kelly, who has blessed me by becoming a second daughter; my sister, Vickie Keen, the person who has been there for me from the start; Vicky Stevens, a forever friend who takes care of me when I forget; my cousin, Shari Morkin, who has not only been my teacher role-model but also my hero; and last, but certainly not least, this is dedicated to my grandson, Wyatt Gale Youngblood—may he be blessed with magnificent teachers that inspire him with their love for literature.

DeLinda Youngblood

We would like to express our appreciation to Dottie Hall for her continual encouragement and valued advice.

DeLinda Youngblood and Eve Hayes

Table of Contents

Table of Contents

Table of Contents

Table of Contents

Introduction

Children's literature is a powerful, multifaceted resource that can enhance classroom instruction in many ways. Books provide enjoyment and entertainment and should be used to demonstrate the marvelous pleasure that reading provides. Books should also be integral components of comprehension strategy and skill instruction. Teachers can use books to provide clear, concrete examples of the kind of thinking that good readers use to construct meaning from text. Stephanie Harvey and Anne Goudvis in *Strategies That Work* (Stenhouse Publications, 2000) refer to these lessons as "anchor experiences." The books that are used as part of strategy and skill instruction become the core books that students can mentally reference to help bridge the gap in their understanding about how effective readers think when constructing meaning from text. This book is designed to link teachers to children's literature that provides strong examples they can use in comprehension mini-lessons.

In Part One, we will review the current thinking of several recognized authorities in the area of reading comprehension in order to provide a quick reference to comprehension strategies and skills. In Part Two, we will share 99 quality children's books that can be helpful models when teaching comprehension strategies and skills. Each featured book includes a synopsis, followed by a selection of strategies or skills that could be taught using the book. Specific examples are cited from the book where the teacher could demonstrate how readers would use particular strategies or skills. These same books may be useful for instruction in strategies and skills in addition to those included in this resource. These books provide strong examples that can greatly enhance students' understanding about how active, engaged readers construct meaning as they read.

It is intended for teachers to use the featured books across grade levels depending on how they are to be incorporated into a lesson. One book could be a wonderful read-aloud in Self-Selected Reading in first or second grade as a model for inferring. That same book could also be a great text for Guided Reading in fifth or sixth grade when students have been scaffolded so that they are ready for independent practice with a particular strategy or skill. For example, the book *Don't Need Friends* by Carolyn Crimi (Random House, 1999) would be great to use as a read-aloud in Self-Selected Reading in second grade to model inferring. Multiple student copies of a Readers' Theater script for the same book would be great for fifth-grade students to practice inferring at the independent level. As you consider the books we have selected, think of how you can use them in your classroom. We offer you a banquet of books . . . come feast!

Comprehension Strategies and Skills

When you teach comprehension, you ask your students to be thoughtful about the texts they are reading. You want them to use the strategies and skills that you teach and model for them. Comprehension strategies provide tactics to derive meaning (Cunningham, Moore, Cunningham, and Moore, 2004).

Most of the leading authorities on reading referenced in this section have identified the same strategies, although there is some divergence regarding how broadly or discreetly these strategies have been identified and grouped. There is little consensus in the research literature on what constitutes a comprehension strategy (Harris and Hodges, 1995). The following is a composite explanation of the strategies most often identified.

In *Guided Reading the Four-Blocks® Way* (Carson-Dellosa Publishing, 2000), Cunningham, Hall, and Cunningham have identified six thinking strategies that readers use to grasp the meaning that the words convey. These strategies are **connecting**, **predicting/anticipating**, **summarizing/ concluding**, **questioning/monitoring**, **imaging/ inferring**, and **evaluating/applying**.

Connecting

As soon as a child starts reading, the process of connecting prior knowledge with the text begins. This is probably the most pervasive thinking strategy a reader uses while reading (Cunningham, Hall, and Cunningham, 2000). Connecting is applied in three areas: text-to-self, text-to-text, and text-to-world. Readers naturally bring their prior knowledge and experience to

reading, but they comprehend better when they think about the connections they make between the text, their lives, and the larger world (Harvey and Goudvis, 2000). Connecting happens before, during, and after reading. Connecting is so integral to reading comprehension that teachers sometimes forget that fledgling readers need some "prompting" to make the personal, world, and intertextual connections that are critical to comprehension (Cunningham, Hall, and Cunningham, 2000).

Predicting/Anticipating

Predicting is a person's use of knowledge about language and the context in which it occurs to anticipate what is coming in writing or speech (Harris and Hodges, 1995). A prediction is an educated guess about what is coming next. The mind thinks ahead about what the text will be about or what may be learned from the text. Predictions are important to reading comprehension because they are one of our brain's ways of actively involving us with our reading (Cunningham, Moore, Cunningham, and Moore, 2004). Good readers also anticipate meaning (Duffy, 2003). Predicting and anticipating keep the reader actively engaged.

Summarizing/Concluding

Summarizing is a brief retelling of an entire text (Duffy, 2003). As a person reads, she constantly accumulates information, and keeps this information in mind by subsuming smaller facts into larger generalizations. The reader summarizes, concludes, infers, and generalizes, and then reads some more, incorporates the new information, and draws even bigger conclusions

(Cunningham, Hall, and Cunningham, 2000). Drawing conclusions and forming generalizations based on facts are of critical importance because these "big ideas" are more easily remembered than the details on which they were based. Generalization is a process in which the brain takes several small pieces of information, and from these small pieces, comes to some larger conclusions (Cunningham, Moore, Cunningham, and Moore, 2004).

Questioning/Self-Monitoring

As a person reads, his brain is constantly monitoring whether what he is reading makes sense. Once a reader realizes that something is not working, he tries some "fix-up" strategies (Cunningham, Hall, and Cunningham, 2000). Self-monitoring is the brain's way of double-checking information. Students are usually aware of the self-monitoring only when they realize that something has gone wrong (Cunningham, Moore, Cunningham, and Moore, 2004). Proficient readers use their questions to clarify and focus their reading (Keene and Zimmermann, 1997). When readers ask questions, they clarify understanding and forge ahead to make meaning. Readers may use a variety of strategies to fix-up comprehension when meaning goes awry (Harvey and Goudvis, 2000). Proficient readers are expected to continually self-monitor and, when needed, to question while they read.

This strategy is not linked to any specific books. Good readers are encouraged to continuously use this strategy anytime they are reading.

Imaging/Inferring

Imaging is the process or result of forming mental images while reading or listening to a story (Harris and Hodges, 1995). When a person reads, she uses all of her senses. When she really gets into what she is reading, she can almost taste, smell, and feel the physical sensations she would actually have if she were in that situation (Cunningham, Hall, and Cunningham, 2000). Proficient readers use these images to deepen their understanding of the text (Keene and Zimmermann, 1997). Based on past experiences, readers create sights, sounds, smells, tastes, and feelings that make books come alive (Cunningham, Moore, Cunningham, and Moore, 2004). Inferring is the ability to understand the meaning an author implies, but does not state directly. Good readers are thoughtfully systematic in using the clues an author supplies and their own background knowledge (Duffy, 2003). Inferring is at the intersection of taking what is known, garnering clues from the text, and thinking ahead (Harvey and Goudvis, 2000). As readers read, they enter the world created by the author. Readers infer why things happen, why characters behave the way they do, and how characters are feeling (Cunningham, Hall, and Cunningham, 2000).

Evaluating/Applying

Evaluating is making judgments about things. When a person evaluates, he compares something to a criterion and sees how it measures up (Cunningham, Moore, Cunningham, and Moore, 2004). The reader makes judgments about what the author is saying (Duffy, 2003). Applying something is using it. When students

apply knowledge to a new situation, they are demonstrating a practical use for what they know (Cunningham, Moore, Cunningham, and Moore, 2004). If after reading a book, a person recommends it to someone, or tells someone about it, or initiates some kind of discussion based on it, he has applied something of the reading to his life (Cunningham, Hall, and Cunningham, 2000).

In addition to utilizing these six thinking strategies to construct meaning, good readers also use their understanding of text structure in order to fully comprehend and enjoy the texts with which they are engaging. Two text structures that readers need to understand are **story structure** and **expository structure**.

Following Story Structure
This strategy requires the reader to identify the characters, setting, plot, and resolution within a text. Good readers have expectations in their minds about what stories include. Following story structure is a comprehension strategy which helps students learn what to expect, and increases their understanding and enjoyment of story reading (Cunningham, Hall, and Cunningham, 2000).

Following Expository Structure
The reader also has expectations when engaging with expository text. She would expect to learn facts and to encounter illustrations, photos, maps, graphs, insets, captions, and other support features usually found in informational text. The most common expository text structures require the reader to determine cause/effect relationships, to compare/contrast information from the text,

and to identify main idea and supporting details (Cunningham, Hall, and Cunningham, 2000).

Many state standards address comprehension strategies as a part of grade-level expectations. In addition, the standards often further articulate these expectations into more discreet facets that could be described as skills.

Strategies, Skills, and Text Features
Strategies are plans that readers use to construct meaning. In comparison, skills are automatic, done without thought (Duffy, 2003). The three differences between strategies and skills are identified by Pearson, Roehler, Dole, and Duffy (1992):

- Students who use strategies are learners with conscious plans for comprehending; students who use skills do so without conscious planning.
- Students become more aware of their reasoning process as they use strategies to make sense out of print; skills seldom involve self-awareness.
- Strategies change with the purpose for reading and the genre being read; skills are not adaptable.

Many of the state standards and grade-level expectations reviewed for this book include the following thinking strategies, skills, and text features.

Characters—a person represented in or acting in a story (Harris and Hodges, 1995)

Setting—the physical and psychological background against which the action in a story takes place, the time and place in which a narrative occurs (Harris and Hodges, 1995)

Plot—the structure of the action of a story (Harris and Hodges, 1995)

Resolution—solution to a conflict in the text

Problem/Solution—a problem is the conflict that arises in the text; the solution is how the conflict is resolved

Sequencing—successive order among ideas or events (Harris and Hodges, 1995)

Cause/Effect—a stated or implied association between an outcome and the conditions that brought it about, often an organizing principle in narrative and expository text (Harris and Hodges, 1995)

Main Idea—what is important; the key idea that is central to the meaning of the text (Harvey and Goudvis, 2000); the gist of a passage; central thought; the chief topic of a passage expressed or implied in a word or phrase (Harris and Hodges, 1995)

Details—pieces of information that support the main idea

Compare/Contrast—a literary technique of placing together like characters, situations, or ideas to show common or contrasting features (Harris and Hodges, 1995)

Author's Purpose (Intent)—the motive or reason for which an author writes, as to entertain, inform, or persuade (Harris and Hodges, 1995)

Figurative Language—language enriched by word images and figures of speech (Harris and Hodges, 1995)

Simile—a comparison of two things that are normally not alike, usually using the words **like** or **as** (for example, The little boy ran as fast as a cheetah.)

Metaphor—a figure of speech in which a comparison is implied by analogy but is not stated (for example, Her eyes were deep pools of blue water.)

Personification—a metaphorical figure of speech in which animals, ideas, objects, etc., are represented as having human qualities (for example, The night breeze whispered secrets from past events.)

Idiom—an expression that does not mean what it literally says (for example, I need help. Could you please give me a hand?)

Hyperbole—an intentionally exaggerated figure of speech (for example, When she won that game, she was ten feet tall and bulletproof.)

Onomatopoeia—words which suggest their meanings through their sounds (for example, He could hear the motorcycle roaring past the house. VARRROOOM!)

Alliteration—repetition of the initial sounds in neighboring words or stressed syllables (for example, Miller makes messy mud pies.)

Context Clues—information from the immediate textual setting that helps identify a word or word group (Harris and Hodges, 1995)

Point of View—the way in which an author reveals his or her voice, as in character, events, and ideas in telling a story (Harris and Hodges, 1995)

Character Analysis—the process by which the reader determines a character's traits and emotions by using information supplied, either explicitly or implicitly, by the author and/or illustrator

Characterization—the way an author presents a character in imaginative writing, as by description, by what the character says, thinks, and does, or by what other characters say, think, or do about the character (Harris and Hodges, 1995)

Picture Clues—illustrations and other page support that help the reader construct meaning of a passage or a specific word

Theme—a major idea or proposition broad enough to cover the entire scope of a piece of literature or other work of art; a theme may be stated or implicit, but clues to it may be found in the ideas that are given special prominence or tend to recur in a work (Harris and Hodges, 1995)

Louise Borden (Scholastic Paperbacks, 2001)
ISBN 0-590-45715-2

A nine-year-old boy is very proud to share his birthday with Abraham Lincoln and takes an even stronger interest in this legend of a man when his classroom teacher points out that they have other things in common besides a birthday. Throughout the book he discovers their many similarities and differences and comes to terms with his own awkwardness of youth.

Ted Lewin incorporates three different media in his illustrations. He utilizes collages, black-and-white drawings, and watercolors to provide a variety of visuals for students.

Use this book to provide an opportunity for students to connect to social studies by asking them to choose a president's life to compare and contrast to their own lives.

Main Idea/Details

★ **Main Idea**—Lincoln had strong hands.
  Details
  • He split rails for a fence.
  • He wrestled two men at a time.
  • He pulled 36 states back together.

★ **Main Idea**—People laughed at Lincoln.
  Details
  • His hair wouldn't comb.
  • He had long, lanky legs.

★ **Main Idea**—People didn't think he'd know how to be president.

Details

- He didn't have "fancy manners."
- He grew up poor.

★ **Main Idea**—Lincoln is on pennies today.

Details

- ". . . he's a hero."
- He freed the slaves.

★ **Main Idea**—I think about Lincoln . . .

Details

- ". . . when I'm the line leader . . . ."
- ". . . when I'm reading books and I don't want them to end . . . ."
- ". . . when I'm singing in the back row. . . ."
- ". . . when I'm out on the playground telling funny jokes and making other kids laugh . . . ."
- ". . . when I'm running from first base to home plate, my team is glad that my legs are long and that my feet are big."

Compare/Contrast

Throughout the book, the boy makes comparisons and contrasts between himself and President Lincoln.

★ **Similarities**

- They share a birthday on February 12.
- They were both tall, skinny, had big hands, big feet, and were clumsy.
- People called them names.

★ **Differences**

- The boy wasn't born in the backwoods of Kentucky.
- His house in the city doesn't have a dirt floor.
- The boy's house has many windows and A. Lincoln's cabin only had one.

Figurative Language

★ **Simile**

- "I think about all those different states, like pieces in a puzzle."
- " . . . I'm as skinny as a beanpole."

★ **Hyperbole**—" . . . and pull 36 states back together." (referring to Lincoln's big hands)

Theme (Implied)

Being happy with who you are and realizing self-worth is more important than one's outer appearance

Carmen Agra Deedy (Peachtree Publishers, 1994)
ISBN 1-561-45096-0

Agatha owned a little shop in Manhattan where she spun her yarn and wove cloth to sell. One evening after work, Agatha went upstairs to her apartment and was anticipating a wonderful night's sleep on her new feather bed. She was sleeping soundly, when suddenly she was awakened by six angry, cold, naked geese at her window. They explained that it is at their expense she was having such a comfortable night's sleep. It was their downy feathers that she was sleeping on. Since she was a caring person she asked them to give her three days to correct her mistake. She then gave them her credit card so they could stay at the Down Town Motel. At the end of three days, the geese returned and found six beautiful warm, white coats that fit each goose perfectly. When asked what she had made them from, they saw she had cut her long, beautiful hair. She explained what was good for the goose was good for the gander and that her hair would grow back as their feathers would. Agatha has not seen the geese since although, someone keeps leaving fresh goose eggs on her step each morning.

Throughout the entire book the puns Deedy uses will "crack" you up and the extra thought put into the illustrations by Laura L. Seeley add additional appeal.

Connecting

Text to World—Students can connect to the importance of giving back to the environment and not just taking away.

Story Structure

★ **Characters**—Agatha, little boy, six geese
★ **Setting**—Agatha's shop, Agatha's apartment
★ **Plot**—After Agatha receives a new feather bed, six geese are very cold because their feathers were used for her bed and they are demanding that their feathers be returned.
★ **Resolution**—Agatha cuts her own long, beautiful hair and weaves it into six warm coats for the geese.

Problem/Solution

★ **Problem**—Agatha, unconsciously, has taken the goose feathers away from the geese so that she can have a more comfortable bed, and now the geese are freezing.
★ **Solution**—Agatha cuts her hair and weaves six warm coats for the geese to wear until their own feathers grow back.

Figurative Language

★ **Simile**—"Her old mattress was so lumpy and bumpy it was like sleeping on coal lumps and cherry pits."

★ **Idiom**
  • "Something in her sensed that her goose was cooked."
  • "Naturally, she'd sent them on a wild goose chase."
  • "'Oh Agatha,'" said one of the geese. "'You keep us in stitches.'"

★ **Hyperbole**—"You could have knocked her over with a feather."

Character Analysis

Agatha proves to be a spontaneous person when she orders a feather bed when she is normally very conscientious about the environment. When she realizes the negative effect she has had by purchasing the down mattress, she takes full responsibility for her actions. She proves she is resourceful by cutting her own hair and making coats for the geese.

Theme (Implied)

Do not take from the environment unless you are prepared to replenish what you take.

Judith Viorst (Aladdin, 1987)
ISBN 0-689-71199-9

Alexander has only bus tokens, while each of his brothers has money. When their grandparents came to visit, they gave Alexander and each of his brothers a dollar. Alexander feels rich and wants to save his money to buy a walkie-talkie, but saving money is hard. There are so many items that lure him to spend his money and he spends his money on these frivolous things. Alexander gets frustrated because his money is disappearing. He says some words that he shouldn't and kicks something. His father "charges" him for this negative behavior and soon all of Alexander's money is gone.

This text has a nice connection to math. Students can calculate how much money each of Alexander's brothers has and can keep a running tally each time Alexander spends or loses money.

Connecting

Text to Text—*Alexander and the Terrible, Horrible, No Good, Very Bad Day* (Aladdin Paperbacks, 1972) and other *Alexander* books by Judith Viorst

Summarizing

This book lends itself well to a retelling.

Story Structure

★ **Characters**—Alexander, Mom, Dad, Nick, Anthony, Grandma Betty, Grandpa Louie
★ **Setting**—Alexander's house, Pearson's Drug Store, Cathy's garage sale
★ **Plot**—Instead of saving, Alexander spends all of his money on frivolous things.
★ **Resolution**—Alexander doesn't have any money, but he does have a deck of cards, a one-eyed bear, and a melted candle.

Main Idea/Details

★ **Main Idea**—Alexander really wants to save his money to buy a walkie-talkie, but loses it or spends it on silly things.

Details—Where does Alexander's money go?

- He buys bubble gum—three times.
- He bets he can hold his breath to the count of 300.
- He bets he can jump from the step and land on his feet.
- He bets he can hide a purple marble.
- He rents a snake for an hour.
- His father fines him for saying certain words.
- He must pay for a candy bar that he ate.
- Nick does a magic trick that makes Alexander's pennies vanish.
- His father makes him pay for kicking.
- He buys a pack of cards.

Annie and the Old One

Miska Miles (Little, Brown and Company, 1985)
ISBN 0-316-57120-2

Annie is very proud of the rug her mother and grandmother are weaving. Then, her grandmother explains that when the rug is completed she will return to Mother Earth. Annie is devastated and puts a plan in place to prevent the rug from being finished. Once her grandmother finds out what is taking place, she shares with Annie the importance of the cycle of life and the love she has for her granddaughter. Understanding her grandmother's words of wisdom, Annie accepts what is to come and learns the art of Navajo weaving. This beautiful book will help children better understand the concept of losing a loved one.

Concluding

There are several examples of conclusions in this book. A few examples are:

★ The tassels on the corn are turning brown.
   Conclusion—It is late summer or early fall.
★ Grandmother tells the family she will go to Mother Earth after the rug is completed.
   Conclusion—She thinks she will die soon.
★ Annie's mother is upset when the sheep are out of the pen.
   Conclusion—She will have to spend her time looking for the sheep instead of weaving.
★ Annie helps Grandmother gather twigs for the hogan.
   Conclusion—They need a fire to heat the hogan.
★ Annie's mother spends a lot of her time weaving rugs.
   Conclusion—Selling rugs is how the family earns a living.
★ Annie brings water to the cornfield and helps watch the sheep.
   Conclusion—Annie has chores she must do every day.
★ Annie can hear everyone breathing as they sleep.
   Conclusion—Everyone in the family sleeps in the same room.

Imaging

Visual—Ask students to visualize the picture in their minds as they read, or you read, the following:

"Annie's Navajo world was good—a world of rippling sand, of high copper-red bluffs in the distance, of the low **mesa** near her own snug **hogan**. The pumpkins were yellow in the cornfield, and the **tassels** on the corn were turning brown."

★ ★ ★ ★ CD-104192 ★ Using Children's Literature to Enhance Reading Instruction

Context Clues

mesa, hogan, tassels, loom, warp, weft, harmony, dawdled, trudged

★ "Annie's Navajo world was good—a world of rippling sand, of high copper-red bluffs in the distance, of the low **mesa** near her own snug **hogan**."

★ "She ran back to the **hogan**, and slithered under her blanket and lay shivering."

★ "The pumpkins were yellow in the cornfield, and the **tassels** on the corn were turning brown."

★ "'My children, when the new rug is taken from the **loom**, I will go to Mother Earth.'"

★ "On the floor of the hogan lay a rug the Old One had woven long, long ago. Its colors were mellowed and its **warp** and **weft** were strong."

★ "She separated the **warp** and the felt for the wool."

★ "'Your grandmother is one of those who live in **harmony** with all nature—with earth, coyote, birds in the sky.'"

★ "When it was time to go to the bus stop to meet the school bus, she **dawdled**, walking slowly and watching her feet."

★ "She hopped down and slowly **trudged** the long way home."

Picture Clues

The pictures will help students have a better visual understanding of particular words in the selection. Ask students to look for the **tassels** on the corn, a **mesa**, a **hogan**, and the weaving **loom**.

Themes (Implied)

★ The cycle of life and coping with the imminent death of a loved one
★ Native American heritage

**Jan Brett (Houghton Mifflin Company, 1989)
ISBN 0-395-51006-6**

Annie is very sad and lonely after her cat, Taffy, disappears on a cold winter day. Annie decides to try and find a new friend. Every day, she places a homemade corn cake at the edge of the woods in hopes of attracting a new pet. The only problem is that the animals the cakes attract (a moose, a wildcat, a bear, and a gray wolf) are not those that Annie sees as appropriate pets. She remains sad and without a new pet throughout the winter. Finally, when spring arrives, Annie gets an unexpected surprise when Taffy comes walking out of the woods with three soft kittens close behind. The sadness of Taffy's disappearance and Annie's lonely days are over.

Jan Brett's exquisite illustration style as the border itself adds a visual perspective to the story.

Predicting/Anticipating

At the beginning of the story, Annie is having difficulty figuring out what is wrong with her cat. Taffy's symptoms are: she has stopped playing, she eats more than usual, she sleeps all day, and she curls up in strange places. Have students make predictions about what is wrong with Taffy.

Summarizing

This text lends itself well to a retelling.

Sequencing

★ Annie's cat Taffy is missing.
★ Annie places a corn cake by the woods.
★ A giant moose comes.
★ Annie places another corn cake by the woods.

- ★ A moose and a wildcat come.
- ★ Annie places more corn cakes by the woods.
- ★ A moose, a wildcat, and a big, growling bear come.
- ★ Annie leaves lots of corn cakes by the woods.
- ★ Several wild animals come.
- ★ Annie runs out of corn cakes.
- ★ The snow melts and spring comes.
- ★ Taffy returns with three kittens.

Picture Clues

Jan Brett uses a delightful border presentation to give the reader a clue of what might occur on the following page. For example, on the page on which the moose is eating, the border surrounding the page reveals the wildcat, which will appear on the next page. On the page where the wildcat is eating, the border features pictures of the bear.

Another visual feature to look for is Taffy hidden in each border. Some of the borders include her kittens, which gives the reader insight to her disappearance.

Arnie the Doughnut

Laurie Keller (Henry Holt and Company, 2003)
ISBN 0-805-06283-1

Arnie the Doughnut was a very proud, chocolate-covered doughnut with bright-colored candy sprinkles. Each day he watched customers choose their favorite doughnuts and leave with them in their paper bags. He anxiously waited to find out who his new owner would be. Finally, Arnie was chosen by a gentleman named Mr. Bing. It was such an exciting day until Arnie realized Mr. Bing wasn't just having him over for a visit but planned on having him for a snack. After talking with Arnie and getting to know him, Mr. Bing decided he couldn't eat him but they would have to find a purpose for Arnie's stay. Together, Arnie and Mr. Bing brainstorm about what else Arnie can be, such as a pincushion, an air freshener, a picture frame, or a paperweight. Finally, after several ideas, they come up with the perfect solution! Mr. Bing has always wanted a dog but he can't have one at his apartment building, so Arnie becomes his pet doughnut.

The illustrations are humorous and, along with text, help to reveal the individuality of each type of doughnut.

Problem/Solution

★ **Problem**—Arnie the Doughnut is about to be eaten by Mr. Bing and Arnie is devastated.

★ **Solution**—Arnie and Mr. Bing decide that since Arnie doesn't want to be eaten and Mr. Bing would like a pet, Arnie will be Mr. Bing's pet doughnut.

Sequencing

The second page shows the sequence of making a doughnut.

★ Cut into a ring
★ Deep-fry
★ Cool
★ Ice
★ Sprinkle
★ Name

Point of View

Arnie shares what "life" is like from the perspective of a doughnut. He shares the experience of when he was first made, the excitement of being chosen from the doughnut case by a customer, and the distress he felt as he realized he was about to be eaten.

★ ★ ★ ★ CD-104192 ★ Using Children's Literature to Enhance Reading Instruction

David Shannon (Scholastic Paperbacks, 2004)
ISBN 0-439-59838-9

Camilla Cream loves lima beans but doesn't want her friends to find out for fear they will make fun of her. In fact, Camilla continually worries about what others think and on the first day of school, her problems begin. She is so concerned with what to wear that she comes down with a bad case of stripes. Camilla's problems escalate as her appearance continues to change to various colors and designs. Even though a variety of doctors, specialists, and experts are brought in, her situation seems hopeless until a very special old woman helps Camilla see the importance of being true to herself.

Connecting

Text to Self—Many children and adults fall into the pattern of attempting to fit in by imitating the likes and dislikes of their peers. In the book, Camilla does not eat lima beans because she is afraid someone might make fun of her for liking them.

Problem/Solution

★ **Problem**—Camilla comes down with a bad case of stripes.
★ **Solution**—A little old lady helps Camilla find that the cure lies in Camilla being true to herself.

Cause/Effect

★ **Cause**—Camilla screams. **Effect**—Her mother runs into Camilla's room.
★ **Cause**—Camilla's mother sees Camilla in bed covered with stripes. **Effect**—Camilla's mother screams.
★ **Cause**—Camilla has a bad case of stripes. **Effect**—Camilla can't go to school.
★ **Cause**—Dr. Bumble can't find any medical problems with Camilla. **Effect**—Camilla is allowed to go back to school.
★ **Cause**—The class says the Pledge of Allegiance. **Effect**—Camilla turns red, white, and blue with stars.

★ **Cause**—Camilla's condition is causing a distraction at school. **Effect**—Camilla's parents are asked to keep her home.

★ **Cause**—Camilla takes her medicine. **Effect**—The next day, Camilla looks like a giant, multi-colored pill.

★ **Cause**—The TV news tells Camilla's story. **Effect**—A huge crowd camps on Camilla's parent's lawn.

★ **Cause**—The Environmental Therapist tells Camilla to become one with her room. **Effect**—Camilla becomes her room.

★ **Cause**—The old woman pops the lima beans into Camilla's mouth. **Effect**—Camilla is cured.

★ **Cause**—Camilla is cured. **Effect**—Camilla eats lima beans whenever she wants and doesn't worry about what her friends might say.

Theme (Implied)

The importance of being yourself

★ ★ ★ ★ CD-104192 ★ **Using Children's Literature to Enhance Reading Instruction**

Baloney (Henry P.)

Jon Scieszka and Lane Smith (Puffin, 2005)
ISBN 0-142-40430-6

The story begins when a little boy (with an alien complexion) named Henry P. Baloney is late for school. His teacher, Miss Bugscuffle, is threatening him with Permanent Lifelong Detention unless he can come up with a very good excuse. His excuse begins when he misplaces his pencil and it escalates into an unbelievable adventure. Miss Bugscuffle is not convinced at the completion of Henry's long-winded excuse. But, since the assignment for the day is to compose a tall tale, she allows him to begin writing because he already has a great tall tale to share. The only problem is, Henry can't find his pencil.

This is where Scieszka and Lane put their creative minds together to come up with an out-of-this-world story. Throughout Henry's exaggerated explanation, the authors substitute words that are not English but come from a variety of languages so that the reader must use context clues to make sense of the story. The great news is that there is a decoder page in the back to decipher all of the unusual words.

Context Clues

This book is excellent for a mini-lesson on using context clues. Below is an example of context clues used to help students decode non-English words used in the text:

"I misplaced my trusty **zimulis**. Then I . . . found it on my **deski**. But someone had put my **deski** in a **torakku**. The **torakku** drove me right here to **szkola**."

Here is the decoded version of this sentence:

I misplaced my trusty **pencil**. Then I . . . found it on my **desk**. But someone had put my **desk** in a **truck**. The **truck** drove me right here to **school**.

Picture Clues

The picture clues, along with the context clues, are extremely important in helping students to construct meaning from the unknown words.

Rosetta Stone (Random House Books for Young Readers, 1975)
ISBN 0-394-83130-6

It all begins with one little bug sneeze. After that, a chain of events starts that can't be stopped. The situation escalates until police officers, a boat, a helicopter, a circus parade, and an entire city are in total chaos. And to think it was all because of one very small bug that sneezed.

Predicting/Anticipating

Once students see the patterns of cause/effect, have them start to predict what might happen next in the story. A few questions might be:

★ What will happen on the page after Jake the turtle falls on his back in the lake?

★ What will happen on the page after the hen kicks the bucket?

★ What will happen to the policeman that flew up all alone?

Cause/Effect

There are several examples of cause/effect in this story. The first few in the book are listed below.

★ **Cause**—A little bug sneezes. **Effect**—A little seed drops.

★ **Cause**—The seed drops. **Effect**—A worm gets hit by the seed.

★ **Cause**—The worm gets hit by the seed. **Effect**—The worm gets mad.

★ **Cause**—The worm gets mad. **Effect**—The worm kicks a tree.

★ **Cause**—The worm kicks a tree. **Effect**—A coconut drops.

★ **Cause**—The coconut drops. **Effect**—A turtle gets bopped.

★ **Cause**—The turtle gets bopped. **Effect**—The turtle splashes into the lake.

★ **Cause**—The turtle splashes into the lake. **Effect**—A hen gets wet.

★ **Cause**—The hen gets wet. **Effect**—The hen gets mad.

David L. Rice (Dawn Publications, 1999)
ISBN 1-883-22089-0

Brian woke up one morning and gave his mother a great, big hug, just because he loved her. This simple act of kindness sets off a series of unselfish acts that touches the lives of many people and animals. The kindness eventually works its way back to Brian.

This book is a wonderful support for character education. There are many opportunities for vocabulary development with the words the author employs to describe how the characters are feeling.

Applying

Treat others kindly so that they will be kind to the people they meet.

Cause/Effect

Every page of the book introduces a new situation in which the kindness from the previous situation causes a reciprocal action on the part of the new character. These are a few of the cause/effect situations from this text:

★ **Cause**—Brian wakes up feeling great. **Effect**—He gives his mother a kiss and hug.

★ **Cause**—Brian's mother feels loved and appreciated. **Effect**—She makes Brian and his sister their favorite breakfast.

★ **Cause**—Brian and Joanna feel loved and cherished. **Effect**—Joanna helps her teacher get ready for school.

★ **Cause**—Mr. Emerson feels competent and successful. **Effect**—He has the class make Ms. Sanchez a banner for her birthday.

★ **Cause**—Ms. Sanchez feels wanted and accepted. **Effect**—She is patient with Loretta.

★ **Cause**—Loretta feels understood. **Effect**—She whispers "XYZ" to Richard.

★ **Cause**—Richard feels relieved. **Effect**—He is supportive of his younger brother.

Bedhead

Margie Palatini (Aladdin, 2003)
ISBN 0-689-86002-1

Oliver shuffles down the hall and into the bathroom. He splashes some water and brushes his teeth. Then, he sees it. It is . . . bedhead. Oliver is having a very bad hair day. His hair is going in every direction. He screams and his family comes running up the stairs and to the bathroom door. Oliver's family urges him to let them into the bathroom. Eventually, he does. Mom, Dad, and Emily try to help. They push it, wet it, spray it, and "hairpin" it, but his hair is still out of control. Against his family's urging, Oliver tries to brush it. The brush gets stuck in the back of his hair. Oliver comes up with a solution: push all of his hair, brush and all, into his old baseball cap. Oliver heads off to school and everything is fine, until a classmate reminds him that today is class picture day and Oliver will not be allowed to wear his cap. When it is picture time, Oliver is directed to remove the cap and everything is fine for a moment. Then, his hair begins to spring out in every direction.

Summarizing

This text lends itself well to a retelling.

Story Structure

★ **Characters**—Oliver, Mom, Dad, Emily, Mary Margaret, Mrs. Oppenheimer, photographer, classmates
★ **Setting**—Oliver's house and the school
★ **Plot**—Oliver's hair was out of control. His family tried to help him, to no avail. He pushed it into a baseball cap only to find that he can't wear the cap for his school picture.
★ **Resolution**—The class picture showed Oliver's hair springing out in every direction.

Problem/Solution

★ **Problem**—Oliver's hair is out of control.
★ **Solution**—The whole family works together to help Oliver. Finally, they all cram his hair into his old baseball cap.

★ ★ ★ ★ CD-104192 ★ Using Children's Literature to Enhance Reading Instruction

Figurative Language

★ **Personification**—"Oliver's scream shook. It rattled."

★ **Hyperbole**—"And there was one teeny, tiny clump of hair way at the back of his head that looked like a cat's coughed-up fur ball."

★ **Onomatopoeia**
  • "Shuffle-shlump, shlumped bleary-eyed Oliver out of bed, down the hall, and into the bathroom."
  • "It dried. B-B-B-Boing! B-Boing! Bink-Bink B-B-B-Boing! Hair started going this way."

Steve Jenkins (Houghton Mifflin Company, 1997)
ISBN 0-395-86136-5

Steve Jenkins takes readers on a trip around the world as he shares some of the world's record-breaking animals. Using comparison charts, students can better understand the size of each record-breaking animal by visually comparing it to something they are familiar with. The book includes a chart naming each animal, what record it has broken, its size, diet, and habitat.

Connecting

★ **Text to Text**—*Hottest, Coldest, Highest, Deepest* by Steve Jenkins (Houghton Mifflin Company, 2004)

★ **Text to World**—Utilizing the chart on the last page and a map, students can locate where the animals can most often be found.

Expository Structure

★ The text is accompanied by illustrations.

★ Illustrations are utilized for comparing size.

★ A chart sharing additional information is included on the last page.

Main Idea/Details

This is an excellent book to read when teaching main idea and details. The main idea for each page is in bold print at the top of the page. The supporting details are in a smaller font elsewhere on the page. A few examples of the main idea and details presented are:

★ **Main Idea**—The African elephant is the biggest land animal.
  Details
  • The largest elephant measured was over 13 feet tall.
  • The largest elephant weighed 22,000 pounds.
  • An African elephant eats over 300 pounds of grass or leaves every day.

★ **Main Idea**—The blue whale is the biggest animal that has ever lived.
  Details
  • The blue whale can grow to be 110 feet long.
  • The blue whale can weigh over 168 tons (as much as 20 elephants).
  • The blue whale is larger than even the biggest dinosaur.

★ **Main Idea**—The biggest snake in the world is the anaconda.

Details

- Anacondas can grow to be over 25 feet long.
- Anacondas can weigh 400 pounds.
- Anacondas wait in trees and drop onto their prey.
- A hungry anaconda can swallow a whole deer, goat, or pig.

Compare/Contrast

The compare and contrast is done visually using a picture of the record-breaking animal and a picture of something the reader will recognize. This helps the reader to better understand the comparison. A few examples are:

★ An elephant and a man
★ The bird spider and a person's hand
★ An electric eel and five light bulbs

Author's Purpose

To inform

Book! Book! Book!

Deborah Bruss (Arthur A. Levine Books, 2001)
ISBN 0-439-13525-7

The farm animals get bored when the children go back to school.
They have no one to play with them. They are depressed and
pouting. The hen decides to take matters into her own hands
and leads the other animals to town to find something to do.
They go to the library to get some books, but the librarian
doesn't understand their requests since their speaking sounds
like "neigh," "moo," "baah," and "oink." Finally, the hen is able
to make herself understood. All of the animals return happily to
the farm. They gather around the books and read until sundown.
Everyone is happy, except the bullfrog, who says, "I already read
it, read it, read it . . . ."

Children enjoy chiming in with the animal sounds in the text. Charming illustrations support the use
of picture clues to enhance understanding.

Summarizing
The text lends itself to a retelling.

Problem/Solution
★ **Problem**—The animals are bored after the children have gone back to school.
★ **Solution**—They go to the library and check out books to enjoy.

Sequencing
★ The children and animals are happy playing together.
★ The animals are bored when the children return to school.
★ The animals head to town to find something to do.
★ They take turns trying to help the librarian understand what they want.
★ The hen is able to make herself understood.
★ They go back to the farm to enjoy the books.
★ The bullfrog is unhappy because he has already read the book.

Picture Clues
★ The library sign indicates where the animals might go in town.
★ The expressions on the animals' faces show their delight when the librarian gives them
  some books.
★ The farm sign indicates where the animals are going when they leave town.

 CD-104192 ★ Using Children's Literature to Enhance Reading Instruction

Mary Hoffman (Puffin, 2000)
ISBN 0-140-55667-2

In this sequel to *Amazing Grace* (Dial Books, 1991), Grace has many questions about families and why hers only has a ma, nana, and a cat named Paw-Paw while others have a mother, a father, a boy, a girl, a dog, and a cat. Meanwhile, her father invites her to visit him and his new family in Africa. Grace and her nana take the trip together, although she is very nervous about meeting her new brother, sister, stepmother, and father that she has not seen since she was very small. The trip proves to be a success as Grace learns to appreciate the difference in customs between Africa and the United States, and forms a strong bond with her father and her new family.

Connecting
★ **Text to Self**
- In books at school, Grace saw that all of the families consisted of a mother and a father, a boy and a girl, and a dog and a cat.
- When Grace met father's new family, she felt they were a "storybook" family because they had a father, mother, brother, sister, and a dog.
- Grace decided her stepmother might be mean because of the stories she had read such as *Cinderella*, *Snow White*, and *Hansel and Gretel*.
- She was telling her new brother and sister stories such as *Beauty and the Beast*, *Rapunzel*, and *Rumpelstiltskin* and reflected on how many stories were about fathers who gave their daughters away.
- Grace compares the tame crocodiles in the holy place to the mean one in *Peter Pan* (J. M. Barrie, Dover Publications, 1999).

★ **Text to Text**—*Amazing Grace* by Mary Hoffman (Dial Books, 1991)

★ **Text to World**—Grace compares where she lives in the United States to her father's home in Africa.

Compare/Contrast
When Grace arrives in Africa she makes comparisons with the United States.
★ **Similarity**
- The Gambia sunshine was like the hottest summer back home.

★ **Differences**
- Sheep wandered the roadside.
- They have different food such as benachin.

- They did their shopping outdoors at the market.
- The money was different and had pictures of crocodiles on it.
- Women carried shopping on their head.
- The clothing was very bright with a variety of patterns.

Figurative Language

★ **Metaphor**—"'I feel like gum, stretched out all thin in a bubble,' she told Nana. 'As if there isn't enough of me to go around. I can't manage two families. What if I burst?'"

Theme (Implied)

★ The author underscores the importance of appreciating the variety in family structures.

★ African American heritage

Bubble Gum, Bubble Gum

Lisa Wheeler (Little, Brown and Company, 2004)
ISBN 0-316-98894-4

The story begins when a fine, fat toad steps in some icky-sticky bubble gum melting in the road and the problem continues from there. As the toad and a whole menagerie of animals get stuck in bubble gum, things can't seem to get worse until a big, blue truck comes their way. To solve the problem, the animals begin chewing and a huge bubble carries them to safety. Then, a big-bottomed bear swats the bubble and a new problem occurs.

Children love the rhythm of the text and the anticipation of what will happen next.

Predicting/Anticipating
★ Who might come along next?
★ Will they be saved from the truck?
★ How might they avoid being hit by the truck?
★ Will the bear get them?
★ What will happen to the big-bottomed bear and the red-ruffled hen?

Sequencing
★ The toad steps in the gum on the road and gets stuck.
★ The shrew gets stuck in the gum.
★ The goose gets stuck in the gum.
★ The bee gets stuck in the gum.
★ The crow gets stuck in the gum.
★ Along comes a truck down the road.
★ The animals chew the gum and blow a bubble.
★ The animals float out of the way of the truck.
★ The bear pops the bubble.
★ The bear gets stuck in the gum.
★ Along comes a red-ruffled hen.

Cause/Effect

★ **Cause**—The animals step in gum. **Effect**—The animals get stuck.

★ **Cause**—A truck drives toward the animals. **Effect**—The animals must blow a bubble and float away to avoid being hit.

★ **Cause**—A bear swats the bubble. **Effect**—The gum falls to the ground.

★ **Cause**—The gum is on the ground. **Effect**—The bear steps in the gum.

★ **Cause**—The bear steps in the gum. **Effect**—The bear gets stuck.

Figurative Language

★ **Onomatopoeia**

- "Splat" (the sound of the toad landing in the gum)
- "Pop! Plop!" (the sound of the bear popping the bubble)

Marilyn Singer (Henry Holt and Company, 1997)
ISBN 0-805-05339-5

Chester lives with a family on a farm where his job is to herd sheep. He loves his job and his sheep. One day, the family decides to move into town. Chester has to leave his sheep and live in the city. Chester is very unhappy and misses his sheep. He gets very bored because he has no work to do. Chester begins to herd things in the city—squirrels, pigeons, delivery men, garbage collectors, firemen, policemen, and an entire girls' softball team. He decides to go back to the farm. On the way home, he comes across some lost sheep that desperately need a shepherd. But, these sheep don't look like his sheep. They don't smell like his sheep, either. They are really lost children dressed up as sheep for a play. Chester shows them the way to school and gets a brand new job as a school crossing guard.

Summarizing

This text lends itself well to a retelling.

Applying

This text helps students to realize the importance of choosing a dog, or any pet, that will be happy in the surroundings to which the animal will be taken.

Story Structure

★ **Main Characters**—Chester, Ma Wippenhooper, Pa Wippenhooper, Claude and Maude Wippenhooper, sheep, children

★ **Setting**—on the farm and in the city

★ **Plot**—A working dog that lives on a farm is transplanted to the city where he has no work to do.

★ **Resolution**—Chester gets a job as a school crossing guard.

Problem/Solution

★ **Problem**—Chester is unhappy because he has lost his job and his sheep.

★ **Solution**—He becomes the school crossing guard, which gives him a new job in the city.

Cause/Effect

★ **Cause**—Chester moves from the country to the city. **Effect**—Chester becomes very unhappy.

★ **Cause**—Chester is bored. **Effect**—Chester begins to herd things in the city.

Author's Purpose

★ To entertain

★ To inform—The author helps children understand the concept that all dogs are not alike. Some dogs are unhappy in situations where other dogs flourish.

Ruth Heller (Putnam Juvenile, 1999)
ISBN 0-698-11778-6

If you would like to know more about the creatures that lay eggs, this is the book for you. You'll learn about chickens, birds, snakes, lizards, crocodiles, turtles, dinosaurs, frogs, toads, salamanders, fish, sea horses, sharks, rays, octopi, moonsnails, spiders, insects, spiny anteaters, and duck-billed platypuses. As you read, you will find interesting details along with information of animal classification.

This is a great support book when studying animal characteristics and classification in science.

Main Idea/Details

There are examples of main idea/details within the text. Two examples are;

★ **Main Idea**—What are amphibians?
   Details
   • When they hatch from eggs, they are called tadpoles.
   • They grow legs.
   • They don't have claws.
   • They don't have scaly skin.

★ **Main Idea**—What are mammals?
   Details
   • They have fur or hair.
   • They nurse their young.
   • They normally don't lay eggs, although there are two exceptions (the spiny anteater and the duck-billed platypus).

Compare/Contrast

Students can compare chickens to other animals that lay eggs.

Similarities—What other animals lay eggs?

- ★ other birds
- ★ most snakes
- ★ lizards
- ★ crocodiles
- ★ turtles
- ★ frogs
- ★ toads
- ★ salamanders
- ★ most fish
- ★ sea horses
- ★ octopuses
- ★ moonsnails
- ★ spiders
- ★ snails
- ★ insects
- ★ spiny anteaters
- ★ duck-billed platypuses
- ★ dinosaurs

Author's Purpose

To inform

Eve Bunting (Voyager Books, 2001)
ISBN 0-152-02407-7

Zoe and her family left her grandparents' farm in Illinois, in a covered wagon, to make new a home in the Nebraska Territory. Zoe's Papa is very excited but her Mama, who is expecting a new baby soon, appears to be quiet and sad about leaving Illinois. Although Zoe and her sister Rebecca are homesick, they want to do something to put a smile on Mama's face. When Zoe sees a group of dandelions growing on the prairie, Papa helps her dig them up as a special birthday surprise for Mama.

This is an excellent book to help build background information when studying Western expansion in the United States.

Inferring

The text is rich for use of inferring. A few examples are:

★ "'But it's so lonely . . . .'" (page 1) What do you think Mama is feeling when she makes this statement?

★ "'We have each other and the girls, and in the fall there will be the new baby.' His voice sounded almost holy. 'A new baby in a new land.'" (page 2) How do you think Papa is feeling when he makes the statement "A new baby in a new land."? Does it help you to make an inference when the author added that Papa almost sounded holy when he spoke?

★ "My little sister Rebecca, put her mouth close to my ear. 'Where are the trees, Zoe?' 'We'll come to some,' I said. We did. But not many." (page 2) Why do you think Rebecca put her mouth close to Zoe's ear to ask the question? How do you think Zoe is feeling when she says, "We did. But not many."?

★ Why does Zoe cry when Papa tells them that the moon and the stars are the same ones that shine over Grandma and Grandpa's house? (page 3)

★ "'We're here!' he called again. I thought this time he was talking to God." (page 5) Share how you think Papa is feeling at this point. Does the punctuation help you to infer?

★ "I will never forget the way Mama looked as she got down from the wagon and stood in the knee-high grass. She shaded her eyes. 'This is where we are going to live our lives?' she asked Papa and her voice was as still as the land around us. 'There is no water.'" (page 6) What do think Mama is feeling as she makes this statement? Why do you think Zoe says she'll never forget the way Mama looked?

Figurative Language

★ **Simile**

- "The sound of the wind in the grass was like the sound of the rivers we'd known back home." (page 3)
- " . . . her voice was as still as the land around us." (page 6)
- "It was true that the soddie did disappear almost as you stepped away from it, turning into just another hump in the ground. 'It's like a prairie dog's burrow,' Mama said." (page 21)

★ **Hyperbole**

- "'We almost dug ourselves a hole into China,' Papa boomed." (page 17)

Character Analysis

Papa is a very optimistic person and is determined that this move will be successful. Throughout the book, his character is shown to be an enthusiastic visionary. Mama, on the other hand, tends to be much more realistic and practical about the trip, focusing on the problems that may arise. She proves to be loyal by making the move with her husband even though she is aware of the probable hardships.

Don't Need Friends

Carolyn Crimi (Dragonfly Books, 2001)
ISBN 0-440-41532-2

Rat and Possum are best friends until Possum moves away to another junkyard leaving Rat behind. Rat decides he doesn't need friends and becomes very mean to the other animals. A new dog moves to the junkyard. He is mean, dirty, and really grouchy. Rat and Dog stay apart, telling each other to stay on his own side. Over time, Rat becomes very accustomed to Dog's howling at night. When it gets really cold, Dog becomes sick and unable to search for food. He stops howling at the moon. Rat drags a sandwich to the front of Dog's barrel, and the two of them become friends. Rat and Dog are now nice to the other animals.

Connecting

★ **Text to Self**—Have students had friends move away?

★ **Text to World**—Have students seen a junkyard?

Inferring

★ "Rat couldn't sleep. He tossed and turned. The quiet was too much for him."
The reader should infer that Rat missed Dog's howling and that's why he couldn't sleep.

★ Dog told Rat not to bring the sandwich this way, but his tail was thumping on the side of his barrel.
The reader should infer that Dog is happy to see the sandwich because he has been sick and unable to hunt for food.

★ Rat and Dog dropped french fries near the smaller animals' homes stating that they hated french fries.
The reader should infer that they were just being nice to the other animals.

Applying

This is a good book to use when encouraging children to befriend a new student that has joined the class.

★ ★ ★ ★ CD-104192 ★ Using Children's Literature to Enhance Reading Instruction

Story Structure

★ **Characters**—Rat, Possum, Dog, other animals in the junkyard (Mouse, Pigeon, Raccoon)

★ **Setting**—a junkyard

★ **Plot**—A lonely rat eventually befriends a dog that has moved into the junkyard.

★ **Resolution**—Rat is no longer lonely. He realizes that he doesn't need many friends, just one.

Theme (Stated)

Friendship

Jerry Pallotta (Charlesbridge Publishing, 2004)
ISBN 0-881-06076-3

Danny has been told that he should not go out in the dory alone, but the ocean is so calm and there are wonderful, interesting creatures to investigate. He decides to row to the big rock in the middle of the bay. From the time Danny leaves shore, marvelous sea creatures begin to surround him. As the creatures get larger and larger, he begins to worry. Danny realizes that he is witnessing the food chain in action. Maybe his mom and dad were right. Perhaps he shouldn't have gone out in the bay alone. He knows that he doesn't want to become a part of the food chain! A tuna smashes into his dory and it capsizes. Danny swims to the rock in the middle of the bay. Just then, he hears his mother's voice telling him that he tells wonderful stories when he is in the bathtub.

This text has a strong connection to science instruction about the food chain/web and to life skills instruction in the area of following rules.

Predicting/Anticipating

★   What will happen to Danny while he is rowing out on the bay?
★   Will Danny survive after his boat capsizes?

Summarizing

This text lends itself well to a retelling.

Applying

We can all tell stories and write them, too.

Story Structure

★   **Characters**—Danny, ocean creatures, Mom
★   **Setting**—the bay, the bathtub
★   **Plot**—A young boy takes the dory out into the bay in spite of his parents' warning that he was too young. He encounters all kinds of sea creatures and gets a good look at the food chain in action.
★   **Resolution**—This exciting adventure is really just Danny's imagination as plays in the bathtub.

Author's Purpose

★   To inform about the food chain
★   To entertain

Context Clues

dory, frenzy, capsized

★ "I pushed the **dory** out and decided to row to the big rock in the middle of the bay."
The illustration of Danny pushing the boat indicates that this is the dory. The previous page told the reader that Danny had been told not to go out in the boat alone.

★ "It was a feeding **frenzy**."
The previous sentence gave the clue that the bluefish were swimming like crazy and eating the mackerels.

★ "Oh, no! I was **capsized**. Thank God I had my life jacket on."

Mary Jane Auch (Holiday House, 1994)
ISBN 0-823-41076-5

Pauline lives in Mrs. Pennywort's henhouse with four other hens. Pauline is not laying any eggs because the hens squabble, and she can't concentrate. Finally, Pauline is able to lay an egg, but it is not like the other eggs. The other hens make fun of her egg even though Pauline thinks it is beautiful. Pauline gets tired of their teasing so she goes outside to lay eggs. She concentrates and stares at the sky; her egg comes out looking like the blue sky with clouds. Mrs. Pennywort sees the egg and loves it. As it turns out, Pauline's eggs come out looking like whatever she sees. Mrs. Pennywort takes Pauline into the house to see what kind of eggs she will lay there. The eggs are so gorgeous that a lady passing by the house asks if Mrs. Pennywort would donate some of the eggs for the town's annual Easter egg hunt. Mrs. Pennywort takes Pauline on field trips for inspiration. On the day that the lady is returning for the eggs, Mrs. Pennywort notices that the eggs on the sunny side of the house are hatching. Mrs. Pennywort plans to give the lady Easter chicks, but Pauline gets very upset. So the lady gets eggs from the shady side of the house and Pauline gets to keep her babies. These chicks grow up to also lay eggs that look like whatever they see.

Predicting/Anticipating
What will Pauline's next egg look like?

Summarizing
This text lends itself well to a retelling.

Story Structure
★ **Characters**—Pauline, Mrs. Pennywort, the other hens, the egg lady
★ **Setting**—Mrs. Pennywort's farm, art museum, and ballet
★ **Plot**—Pauline lays eggs that look like what she sees. Her eggs are donated for the annual Easter egg hunt, but some of them begin to hatch.
★ **Resolution**—The egg lady gets the eggs from the shady side of the house.

Problem/Solution

★ **Problem**—The eggs on the sunny side of the house begin to hatch. How will Mrs. Pennywort supply the eggs for the egg hunt?

★ **Solution**—Mrs. Pennywort gets the eggs from the shady side of the house.

Theme (Implied)

It's okay to be different.

Julie Danneberg (Charlesbridge Publishing, 2000)
ISBN 1-580-89061-X

Sarah doesn't want to go to school. It is her first day at a new school and she is really anxious. She tells Mr. Hartwell that she is not going and gives all kinds of excuses. Mr. Hartwell insists that she must go to school. Everyone is expecting her. He drives her to school where she is met by the principal who leads Sarah to her new classroom. It is only when they arrive and the principal introduces Sarah to the class that the reader discovers that Sarah is the teacher.

Connecting

Text to Self—Ask students, "How do you feel on the first day of school?" Some students may have started at a new school.

Summarizing/Concluding

★ **Summarizing**—This text lends itself to a retelling.

★ **Concluding**—Who is Mr. Hartwell? The text doesn't indicate. Some readers may conclude that Mr. Hartwell is Sarah's husband; others may conclude that Mr. Hartwell is Sarah's father.

Story Structure

★ **Characters**—Sarah, Mr. Hartwell, Mrs. Burton, students

★ **Setting**—the Hartwell's house, the school

★ **Plot**—Sarah doesn't want to begin at a new school, but is coaxed into going by Mr. Hartwell.

★ **Resolution**—Sarah is the new teacher, not the new student.

Sequencing

★ Sarah doesn't want to go to school.

★ Mr. Hartwell convinces her that she must.

★ Mrs. Burton leads Sarah to class.

★ Mrs. Burton introduces Sarah as the new teacher.

Gasp! The Breathtaking Adventures of a Fish Left Home Alone

Terry Denton (Penguin Global, 2004)
ISBN 0-140-55700-8

It all begins with a fish that is left alone. He decides to get some extra fish food but accidentally falls out of his bowl. He must quickly find a water supply or expire. Each time that he thinks he has solved his problem something gets in his way.

This page-flipping, countdown text is filled with drama and suspense. The text presentation is an effective way to encourage students to read with expression.

Connecting

Text to Text—*The Monster at the End of This Book* by Jon Stone (Random House Children's Books, 2004)

Predicting/Anticipating

Have the students predict what will happen with each of the new ideas that the fish tries. A few questions might be:

★ Will the fish survive?

★ If yes, how will he find water?

★ What will happen when he gets in the sink? (page 26)

★ What will happen as the fish vaults towards the toilet? (page 20)

Summarizing

This text lends itself to a retelling.

Cause/Effect

★ **Cause**—The fish tries to get fish food by himself. **Effect**—He falls out of the fish bowl.

★ **Cause**—The fish goes to the sink to get water. **Effect**—There isn't any water in the sink.

★ **Cause**—There isn't any water in the sink. **Effect**—The fish goes to the toilet.

★ **Cause**—The fish uses the toilet brush to attempt to get into the toilet bowl. **Effect**—Someone put plastic wrap over the toilet bowl so he bounces off.

Picture Clues

The illustrations display the fish's emotions throughout the book. A few examples are:

★ Excitement—when he grabs the fish food

★ Fear—when his bowl falls

★ Terror—when his bowl breaks

★ Pride—when he does a triple somersault with pike into the toilet

The Giant Hug

Sandra Horning (Knopf Books for Young Readers, 2005)
ISBN 0-375-82477-4

Owen decides that for his Granny's birthday, he wants to send her a giant hug through the mail. Although it is an unusual request, the post office goes beyond their normal delivery procedures as the postal workers put a little joy in one another's day by passing on Owen's hug. It passes from animal to animal, by truck, plane, and mail carrier making for a delightful day for all who give and receive the hug. When Shelly, the mail carrier, delivers Owen's birthday hug to Granny, Granny is so excited she sends a kiss right back to Owen in the mail. Here we go again!

Connecting

Text to Self—Ask students:

- Do you send mail to a grandparent or relative that lives far away?
- Have you ever given a hug that made someone feel better?
- Have you ever received a hug that made you feel better?

Sequencing

★ Owen and his mother take his hug to the post office.
★ Owen gives his hug to Mr. Nevins at the post office.
★ Mr. Nevins gives the hug to Ms. Porter who sorts the mail and puts it on the truck.
★ Ms. Porter gives the hug to Leroy who drives the mail to the city.
★ Leroy gives the hug to James who drives the mail from the city to the airport.
★ James gives the hug to Captain Johnson who will fly the mail airplane.
★ Captain Johnson gives the hug to Amanda who will drive the truck from the airport to the city.
★ Amanda gives the hug to Chad who will deliver the mail to Granny's town.
★ Chad gives the hug to Ms. Greenburg the supervisor at the post office in Granny's town.
★ Ms. Greenburg gives the hug to Shelly who is the mail carrier who delivers Granny's mail.
★ Shelly gives Granny the giant hug from Owen.
★ Granny gives Shelly a kiss to send back to Owen.

Cause/Effect

★ **Cause**—Mr. Nevin gave Ms. Porter the hug. **Effect**—Ms. Porter smiled as she sorted the mail.
★ **Cause**—Ms. Porter gave Leroy the hug. **Effect**—Leroy whistled all of the way to the city.
★ **Cause**—Amanda gave Chad the hug. **Effect**—Chad asked Amanda to go out dancing.
★ **Cause**—Amanda said she'd love to go dancing with Chad. **Effect**—Chad kicked up his heels and hopped in his truck.

Giggle, Giggle, Quack

Doreen Cronin (Simon & Schuster Children's Publishing, 2002)
ISBN 0-689-84506-5

Farmer Brown goes on vacation and leaves his brother Bob in charge. Farmer Brown has carefully written out instructions for the animals' care. Farmer Brown warns Bob about Duck, saying that Duck is trouble. Duck changes all of the instructions to notes that the animals would like better. He has Bob order pizza for all the animals, wash the pigs in Farmer Brown's favorite bubble bath, and play movies for the animals. Farmer Brown calls to check in on things at home. All he hears is the happy sounds of the animals as they are watching the movie. Farmer Brown hurries home.

Connecting

Text to Text—*Click, Clack, Moo: Cows That Type* by Doreen Cronin (Simon & Schuster, 2000)

Summarizing/Concluding

★ **Summarizing**—This text lends itself to a retelling.

★ **Concluding**—Do these notes sound like logical instructions Farmer Brown would leave for the animals' care? Since these sound like unusual directions and Duck is often seen with paper and pencil, the reader should conclude that Duck is changing the notes.

Story Structure

★ **Characters**—Farmer Brown, Bob, Duck, other farm animals
★ **Setting**—the farm
★ **Plot**—Farmer Brown goes on vacation and leaves Bob in charge. Duck changes all of the instructions that Farmer Brown left.
★ **Resolution**—Farmer Brown has to hurry home.

Picture Clues

★ Duck sees a pencil on the ground as Farmer Brown drives off.
★ Several pages show Duck with a pencil and sometimes with a pencil and paper.
★ On the page that shows Bob talking on the phone to Farmer Brown, Duck is sharpening a pencil.
★ The illustration on the last page shows Farmer Brown hurrying home.

Giles Andreae (Orchard Books, 2001)
ISBN 1-841-21565-1

Gerald the giraffe is very nervous because it is time for the big jungle dance. Although he is very good at several things, dancing is not one of them. All of the other animals seem to know just what to do as they dance the tango, waltz, cha-cha, and Scottish reel. As the dance begins and the animals dance so well, poor Gerald musters up his courage and walks onto the dance floor. All of the animals make fun of him and say extremely cruel things to poor Gerald. As Gerald sadly walks back home, a cricket speaks to him. He tells Gerald that sometimes when you're different you just need to hear a different song—listen to the sounds around you in nature. As Gerald listens, his body starts swaying and before you know it, he is dancing. The other animals are amazed at Gerald's transformation. Gerald realizes that everyone can dance when they find music that they love.

Connecting

★ **Text to Self**—Ask students, "Have you ever had a time that you felt you didn't fit in or someone made fun of you? Have you ever made fun of someone else?"

★ **Text to Text**—*Finklehopper Frog* by Irene Livingston (Tricycle Press, 2003)

Summarizing
This text lends itself well to a retelling.

Applying
This is a great book to use when discussing acceptance and reflecting on what students' behavior should be towards others.

Problem/Solution

★ **Problem**—Gerald doesn't fit in with the rest of the animals and they make fun of him because he can't dance.

★ **Solution**—Gerald learns that you just need to hear your own music and be an individual to be at your best.

Give Maggie a Chance

Frieda Wishinsky (Fitzhenry & Whiteside Limited, 2002)
ISBN 1-550-41682-0

Maggie has a problem—she is shy. She would love to be able to read in front of the class or to speak up and solve math problems for the teacher, but her shyness is holding her back. She becomes so embarrassed that she imagines the floor swallowing her or being blasted to Mars. Her friend Sam, who encourages her, also has a problem—he stutters. To make matters worse, they have Kimberly in their class. Kimberly volunteers for everything and brags continuously. When Kimberly is being mean, Maggie imagines Kimberly being carried away by a giant bird or being dumped into a dungeon by a troll. The day Kimberly makes fun of Sam is the day that Maggie forgets her shyness and stands up for her friend. Just like magic, her fear of Kimberly is gone and all that she sees when she is in front of the class is Sam smiling.

Connecting

★ **Text to Self**—Ask students, "Have you ever felt like any of the characters in the story? Have you ever felt shy? Have you ever bragged? Have you ever been impatient? Have you ever been a good friend? Have you ever wished you had been somewhere other than where you were? Have you wished someone had been somewhere else? Have you ever encouraged someone to do something you knew they were scared to do?"

★ **Text to Text**—*Simon Can't Say Hippopotamus* by Bonnie Highsmith Taylor (Mondo Publishing, 2003)

Imaging/Inferring

★ **Imaging**—This text lends itself well to imaging as Maggie uses creative possibilities for ridding herself of her embarrassment and Kimberly. Invite students to close their eyes and make pictures in their mind of the following:
  • "Maggie wanted the floor to swallow her up."
  • "Maggie wanted a rocket to blast her to Mars."
  • "Maggie wanted a genie to make the class disappear."
  • "Maggie wished a giant wave would wash Kimberly out the door."
  • "She wished a giant bird would fly Kimberly out the window."
  • "She wished a giant troll would dump Kimberly into a dungeon."
  • "It was as if a magician had whisked Kimberly away."

- "It was as if a witch had poofed her to smoke."
- "It was as if a wizard had turned her into a small, warty toad."

★ **Inferring**—This book is strong for inferring the character's feelings. After reading the following sentences, discuss how the characters felt:
  - "Maggie leaped out of bed. She slipped on her new dress and spun like a ballerina in her new shoes. She skipped all the way to her new class."
  - "Maggie opened her mouth but nothing came out. Not a word. Not a sound. Not even a whisper."
  - "'Let me read! Let me read!' shouted Kimberly, leaping out of her seat." (How do you think this makes Maggie feel?)
  - "Kimberly tapped Maggie on the shoulder. 'Reading is SO easy,' said Kimberly. 'I've been reading since I was a baby.'" (How do you think this statement makes Maggie feel?)
  - "'Tomorrow I'll read like that to my class,' she told herself."
  - "'Maggie,' said Mrs. Brown. Maggie opened her mouth to read. But nothing came out." (How do you think Maggie feels? How do you think Mrs. Brown feels?)
  - "'I'll read tomorrow.' She promised herself. 'I won't let anything stop me.'"
  - "'What's the matter with you?' snickered Kimberly. 'Can't you talk?'" (How do you think Kimberly was feeling when she said this? How do you think Sam felt when Kimberly said this to him? How do you think Maggie felt when Kimberly said this to her friend Sam?)
  - "Maggie saw only her friend Sam. Sam was smiling at her."

Applying

If you know a person that someone makes fun of, you could be a good friend like Maggie and stand up for them.

Problem/Solution

★ **Problem**—Maggie is too shy to share.
★ **Solution**—When Kimberly makes fun of Sam and Maggie stands up for her friend, she forgets all about her shyness.

Figurative Language

★ **Simile**
  - "Her heart thumped like a drum."
  - "Her knees quivered like jelly."
  - "Her mouth was as dry as a desert."
  - "Like a nightmare, it wouldn't end."

- "Maggie's face turned as red as a radish."
- "Like a toothache it wouldn't end."
- "Maggie's heart sunk as Kimberly flapped her hands in the air like a seagull."

★ **Personification**—"Maggie wanted the floor to swallow her up."

Theme (Implied)
Overcoming a fear

Grandpa's Teeth

Rod Clement (HarperTrophy, 1999)
ISBN 0-064-43557-1

Grandpa's teeth are missing. The family searches everywhere, but to no avail. Finally, the police are called to the crime scene. Wanted posters are put up along with a police artist's picture of the missing teeth. Everyone becomes a suspect, especially those who do not smile. There is a police line-up and Grandpa gets interviewed for the TV program, *Unsolved Crimes*. As a result, the whole town begins to smile broadly. This scares the tourists who stop coming to visit, so all of the shop owners begin to lose business. A town meeting is held and a collection is taken to replace the teeth. Enough money is collected to order two sets of teeth. Soon the new teeth arrive. Grandpa smiles broadly showing off his new teeth. So does his dog, Gump, who smiles for the first time ever. The surprise ending is that Gump has Grandpa's old teeth in his mouth.

Predicting/Anticipating
Where are the missing teeth?

Summarizing
This text lends itself well to a retelling.

Story Structure
★ **Characters**
- **Major Characters**—Grandpa, Mom, Officer Rate
- **Minor Characters**—Agatha, boy, tourists, police artist, Mrs. Carbuncle, townspeople, mayor

★ **Setting**—Grandpa's house, the town

★ **Plot**—Grandpa loses his teeth. He thinks someone has stolen them and is suspicious of everyone.

★ **Resolution**—The whole town contributes to the effort to replace the teeth. Eventually, the missing teeth are found in Gump's mouth.

Problem/Solution
★ **Problem**—The town is suffering due to Grandpa's missing teeth.

★ **Solution**—The townspeople work together to take up a collection to buy a new set of teeth for Grandpa.

Cause/Effect

★ **Cause**—Everyone in town begins to smile broadly all the time. **Effect**—The tourists are frightened.

★ **Cause**—The tourists stop visiting the town. **Effect**—The shops lose business.

Picture Clues

The picture on the last page reveals the location of Grandpa's missing teeth—in Gump's mouth.

Tedd Arnold (Puffin, 1998)
ISBN 0-140-56362-8

Wilma wakes up one morning with a new green complexion and a strange desire to do things she has never done before, such as eat flies and bugs and jump out of windows. Her day at school proves to be very interesting as she dives in the fish aquarium, tries to get a fly off her teacher's nose with her tongue, and chases the fly through the school creating complete chaos. The ending is a complete surprise when you find that everything is only a little frog's dream.

Summarizing
This text lends itself well to a retelling.

Compare/Contrast
Have students list what similarities they see between Wilma and a frog. Here are a few examples:

★ **Similarities**
- She is green.
- She croaks.
- She eats flies and bugs.
- She hops.

★ **Differences**
- She sleeps in a bed.
- She wears clothes.
- She has hair.
- She makes her bed.
- She eats at a table in her house.
- She is a student at school.

Picture Clues

The picture clues support the reader with visuals of Green Wilma's frog-like characteristics within the setting of the lifestyle of a child. Here are a few examples:

★ Wilma in her bedroom—sitting like a frog on her pillow, leaping out of bed after a fly, making her bed in an unusual manner

★ Wilma in her bathroom—sitting in water in the sink combing her hair)

★ Wilma in her kitchen—her appearance is very different from that of her family

★ Wilma leaving her house—she jumps out of the window instead of using the door to get to the school bus

★ Wilma riding the bus—she sits on the driver's head

Jane Breskin Zalben (Dutton Juvenile, 2005)
ISBN 0-525-47097-2

The old woman who lives in a shoe and her family have a problem. They have outgrown their shoe and ask Mother Goose for help. Mother Goose begins moving all of the residents of Fairy Tale Land. The old woman and her family move into Snow White's cottage. Snow White and the dwarfs move into Rapunzel's castle and the moving continues until the old woman and her children begin to realize that there's no place like a shoe. As the old woman yells that it's time to go back, everyone packs their belongings to return to their original homes, all the while trying to remember why they ever left in the first place.

This rhyming text is a delightful way to review nursery rhymes and fairy tales.

Connecting

★ **Text to Self**—Ask students, "Have you ever wished that you could be somewhere else but after being there awhile, you were ready to return home?"

★ **Text to Text**—This is a great book to connect to nursery rhymes and fairy tales.

Problem/Solution

This text has problem/solution examples throughout. Here are a few examples:

★ **Problem**—The home of the old woman who lived in the shoe was getting too small.

★ **Solution**—Her family moved into the home of Snow White and the seven dwarfs.

★ **Problem**—Rapunzel's hair was a hassle.

★ **Solution**—She rented a room from Rumpelstiltskin who said he could spin her hair into gold.

★ **Problem**—Rumpelstiltskin was tired of spinning Rapunzel's hair into gold.

★ **Solution**—He moved to the cottage of Hansel and Gretel.

★ **Problem**—Hansel and Gretel have eaten so many sweets that their clothes will not fit.

★ **Solution**—They jog to a garden and eat parsley, lettuce, and beans.

Sequencing

★ The old woman and her family moved to Snow White's cottage.

★ Snow White and the dwarfs moved to Rapunzel's castle.

★ Rapunzel rented a room from Rumpelstiltskin.

★ Rumpelstiltskin moved to Hansel and Gretel's cottage.

★ Hansel and Gretel went to the garden to eat greens.

- ★ Jack and Jill went to live at the home of one of the three little pigs.
- ★ The three little pigs moved to Sleeping Beauty's castle.
- ★ Sleeping Beauty moved to the home of the three bears.
- ★ The three bears moved into the old woman's shoe.

Figurative Language

Simile—"Why, our shoe is enormous!" the Old Woman said as her children lay squeezed like sardines in their beds.

The Honest-to-Goodness Truth

Patricia C. McKissack (Aladdin, 2003)
ISBN 0-689-85395-5

Libby lies to her mother about feeding and watering the horse. It is so easy to lie, but her mother finds out the truth and Libby is punished double. Libby decides to tell only the whole truth from now on. She tells Ruthie Mae that she has a hole in her sock. Libby tells the teacher that Willie didn't do his geography homework. After hurting her friends, and several other people, Libby comes to understand that it is not necessary to blurt out the whole truth all of the time. Libby makes amends with those she has wounded with her words.

Summarizing
This text lends itself well to a retelling.

Applying
We can be honest without being hurtful.

Story Structure
★ **Characters**—Libby, Mama, Ruthie Mae, Willie, classmates, Miz Jackson, Miz Tusselbury, Virginia Washington
★ **Setting**—Libby's house, church yard, school, Miz Tusselbury's yard
★ **Plot**—Libby lies and is punished. She vows to tell only the whole truth from then on. She hurts several people with her brutal honesty.
★ **Resolution**—She learns that the truth doesn't have to be hurtful.

Cause/Effect
Cause—Libby is brutally honest. **Effect**—Libby hurts her friends' feelings and they become angry with her.

Figurative Language

★ **Simile**

- "She was surprised at how easy the lie slid out of her mouth, like it was greased with warm butter."
- "Libby's stomach felt like she'd swallowed a handful of chicken feathers."
- "'Miz Tusselbury, truly and honestly, your yard looks like a . . . a . . . a jungle.'"
- "Willie was mad as a hornet when I told Miz Jackson he didn't have his homework."

★ **Hyperbole**

- "That horse is older than black pepper."

Themes

★ Sometimes the truth needs to be tempered with compassion. (stated)

★ African American heritage

Helen Lester (Houghton Mifflin Company, 2002)
ISBN 0-618-21612-X

Rodney Rat can't pronounce his r's. He is teased by the other rodents at school. A large, mean rodent moves into the school. All of the students are afraid of her. Rodney is chosen to be the leader of "Simon Says." He is terrified of Camilla's reaction when she hears him speak. Since Camilla is unaware of Rodney's speech impediment, she follows his instructions in "Simon Says" exactly as they sound. Rodney says to "weed" the sign. Camilla pulls up the weeds around the sign instead of "reading" the sign. Finally, Rodney tells everyone to go "west." Camilla interprets this as an instruction to head west instead of go "rest." Rodney becomes the hero for having rid the school of the bully.

Connecting

Text to Self—Some students will have experienced the cruelty of a bully.

Summarizing

This text lends itself well to a retelling.

Story Structure

★ **Characters**—Rodney Rat, classmates, Camilla, Miss Fuzzleworth
★ **Setting**—classroom, playground
★ **Plot**—Rodney has a speech problem and is teased by the other rodents. He is worried about leading a "Simon Says" game.
★ **Resolution**—He becomes the hero of the class by giving directions that rid the school of a new bully who has moved into the class.

Cause/Effect

★ **Cause**—The other rodents tease Rodney. **Effect**—He is shy, soft-spoken, and eats lunch alone.
★ **Cause**—Camilla doesn't know about Rodney's speech problem. **Effect**—She follows his directions exactly.

Theme (Implied)

We all have strengths.

Hottest, Coldest, Highest, Deepest

Steve Jenkins (Houghton Mifflin Company, 2004)
ISBN 0-618-49488-X

Take a trip around the world with Steve Jenkins as he shares the most incredible facts on Earth. Readers will learn about the longest river, oldest and deepest lake, highest mountain, hottest and windiest spots, coldest, wettest, and driest places, highest waterfall, deepest spot, most active volcano, most extreme tides, and the snowiest place.

This nonfiction book is filled with interesting facts and details with graphs that allow the reader to visually compare and contrast. Jenkins's paper collage illustrations add to the enjoyment of the book.

Connecting

★ **Text to Text**—*Biggest, Strongest, Fastest* by Steve Jenkins (Houghton Mifflin Company, 1997)
★ **Text to World**—Have students travel the world by finding these record-breaking places on a map.

Expository Structure

★ Maps
★ Bold print for important words
★ Graphs utilizing compare/contrast with text and illustrations

Main Idea/Details

Many details are listed throughout the book. Here are some examples:

★ **Main Idea**—Lake Baikal, in Russia, is the world's oldest and deepest lake.
   Details
   • It was formed about 25 million years ago.
   • "In one spot it is 5,134 feet deep."
   • It contains more water than all five Great Lakes combined.

★ **Main Idea**—Sangay, in Ecuador, is the world's most active volcano.
   Details
   • From 1937 to 1998 (when the book was published), it had erupted an average of once every 24 hours.
   • "It once erupted more than 400 times in a single day."

Compare/Contrast

This book is filled with examples of compare/contrast both in illustrations and in text. Here are a few examples:

★ Nile River (4,145 miles)
   Mississippi River (3,710 miles)
★ Mt. Everest (29,028 feet)
   Empire State Building (1,250 feet)
★ Tutunendo, Columbia (463 inches average annual precipitation)
   Chicago, IL (36 inches average annual precipitation)

Author's Purpose

To inform

A House for Hermit Crab

Eric Carle (Aladdin, 2002)
ISBN 0-689-84894-3

Hermit Crab has outgrown his shell and has found a new one. Each month he travels along the ocean floor and invites various sea creatures to help decorate his shell. He finds positive qualities that each creature has to share to make his new home a better place to live. In November, Hermit Crab discovers that he is outgrowing his shell. Although he knows that he needs to move on, he is sad about leaving his new friends. Moving becomes easier when a smaller hermit crab asks him for help in finding a home. Hermit has the perfect place for him. Then, Hermit moves to a larger shell that is ready for a makeover.

This is a wonderful book to share with students if they are dealing with moving to a different classroom, grade level, house, location, etc. Integrated into the text are facts concerning creatures on the ocean floor. The last page of the book is a marine life glossary.

Connecting

★ **Text to Self**—Many students have some type of connection with moving—to a different classroom, grade level, house, community, etc. Use this book as a great resource for beginning conversations about students' feelings when they had to move.

★ **Text to World**—Discuss oceans and the plants and animals that live there.

Expository Structure
Marine life vocabulary is defined in the back of the book.

Sequencing
The book takes readers through the year with Hermit Crab.

★ January—Hermit outgrows his small shell.
★ February—Hermit finds a larger shell for a home.
★ March—The sea anemones go to live with Hermit.
★ April—The sea star goes to live with Hermit.
★ May—The coral goes to live with Hermit.
★ June—The snail goes to live with Hermit.
★ July—The sea urchin goes to live with Hermit.
★ August — Hermit and his friends go through the dark forest of seaweed.
★ September—The lanternfish swim over Hermit's shell to light his way.
★ October—Hermit builds a pebble wall to go around his shell.

★ November—Hermit discovers that his shell is getting too small for him.

★ December—Hermit offers his too-small shell to a smaller crab who has outgrown his shell.

★ January—The smaller crab moves into Hermit's shell and Hermit moves out and finds a larger shell.

Cause/Effect

Here are a few examples of cause/effect:

★ **Cause**—Hermit the Crab has outgrown his shell. **Effect**—He leaves his old shell and finds a new, larger one.

★ **Cause**—Hermit's shell looks plain. **Effect**—He invites sea creatures to help him decorate it.

★ **Cause**—Hermit wanders into a forest of dark seaweed. **Effect**—It is so dark he can hardly see.

★ **Cause**—The lanternfish swim over Hermit in the dark water showing off a bright light. **Effect**—Hermit invites them to swim over his shell to light up his home.

Author's Purpose

★ To entertain

★ To inform

Theme (Implied)

Moving and change

Robin Michal Koontz (Millbrook Press, 2002)
ISBN 0-761-32669-3

How is a honeybee like a manatee? Would you like to know what a cockatoo and a kangaroo have in common? The author shares ways these animals are different and then what the unlikely pair have in common. This is a fun book filled with animal facts.

Connecting

★ **Text to World**—Students may use the information on pages 30 and 31 to locate the animals' locations on a map.

Expository Structure

★ Animal facts are listed on the last two pages.

★ The text is filled with comparisons of animals.

Main Idea/Details

Many details are listed throughout the book, and additional facts are listed in the back. Here are some examples:

★ **Main Idea**—Bullfrogs
   Details
   • They live in wet places.
   • They live in North America.
   • They like mud.
   • They have no hair.
   • They have long toes for swimming and jumping.

★ **Main Idea**—Cockatoos
   Details
   • They live in Australia and surrounding islands.
   • They can live to be over 70 years old.
   • They have claws for climbing.
   • They build nests for their babies.
   • They live in groups called flocks.
   • "They like to live in trees."

 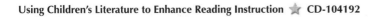

Compare/Contrast

This text is filled with compare/contrast. Here are a few examples:

★ **Similarity**—a moose and a goose
  • A moose and a goose both like to eat plants.
★ **Differences**—a moose and a goose
  • "A moose is tall." "A goose is short."
  • "A moose is fuzzy." "A goose has feathers."
  • A moose doesn't make much noise. A goose makes a lot of noise.
★ **Similarity**—a honeybee and a manatee
  • A honeybee and a manatee both like to dance with friends.
★ **Differences**—a honeybee and a manatee
  • A honeybee flies. A manatee swims.
  • A honeybee makes a buzzing noise. A manatee makes a swishing sound.
  • A honeybee's dance tells a story of where to find flowers. A manatee's dance is like playing "Follow the Leader."
★ **Similarity**—a gorilla and a chinchilla
  • A gorilla and a chinchilla both live in big families that like to nest together.
★ **Differences**—a gorilla and a chinchilla
  • "A gorilla is huge." "A chinchilla is small."
  • "A gorilla is hairy." "A chinchilla is fluffy."
  • A gorilla sometimes beats its chest. A chinchilla never beats its chest.
★ **Similarities**—a sloth and a moth
  • "A sloth often hangs upside down." "A moth can also hang upside down."
  • A sloth almost never makes a sound. A moth never makes a sound.
★ **Differences**—a sloth and a moth
  • "A sloth is slow." "A moth is fast."
  • "A sloth is lazy." "A moth is lively."
  • A sloth spends most of its life being still. A moth spends most of its time on the move.

Author's Purpose

★ To entertain
★ To inform

Brigitte Luciani (North-South Books, 2000)
ISBN 0-735-81269-1

One summer day, Roxanne decides to go to the beach. She wants to take five things with her: her turtle, umbrella, thick book of stories, a ball, and her baby. But, Roxanne immediately has a problem because her car won't start. So, she decides to ride the bus. As Roxanne and her baby start to board the bus, the driver informs them that animals can't ride the bus so they have to make a new plan. Throughout the entire book, Roxanne has difficulty finding transportation to take everything to the beach.

This is a fun visual guessing game for children as they try to use picture clues to see what is missing in each picture.

Predicting/Anticipating
Have students predict how they think Roxanne will try to get to the beach after each failed attempt.

Problem/Solution
★ **Problem**—Each mode of transportation that Roxanne chooses can't accommodate all five things that she wants to take with her to the beach.

★ **Solution**—She continues to try to find a solution and after several attempts, her persistence pays off as she rides with a farmer in his cart. She has a lovely day at the beach with her turtle, ball, umbrella, book, and, of course, her baby.

Sequencing
• Roxanne's car won't start.
• Roxanne tries to ride the bus.
• Roxanne decides to ride her bike.
• Roxanne starts off on her skateboard.
• Roxanne gets in the kayak.
• Roxanne attempts to go in the hot air balloon.
• Roxanne rides with the farmer.
• They have a wonderful time at the beach.

Cause/Effect
★ **Cause**—The turtle can't ride because animals aren't allowed on the bus. **Effect**—They can't ride the bus.

★ **Cause**—The ball won't fit on the bike. **Effect**—They can't ride the bike.

- ★ **Cause**—Roxanne's hands are too full to hold the umbrella. **Effect**—They can't ride on the skateboard.
- ★ **Cause**—The kayak is wobbly and the book might get wet. **Effect**—They can't take the kayak.
- ★ **Cause**—The baby is afraid of flying. **Effect**—They can't go in the hot air balloon.

Character Analysis

Roxanne is a very persistent young lady who never gives up even though there is a problem each time she chooses a different mode of transportation. She tends to be a flexible person who is always ready to look for an alternative way to get to the beach and is good-natured even through difficult times.

Picture Clues

The pages in the book alternate. On one page, students must look to see which of Roxanne's five things could not go. On the following page is an explanation as to why the item couldn't travel on that particular mode of transportation.

Karen Beaumont (Harcourt Children's Books, 2005)
ISBN 0-152-02488-3

Be prepared to read this delightful book multiple times. Children love David Catrow's fun illustrations and the toe-tapping rhythm of the rhyming text. After becoming frustrated with finding paint on the floor, and the ceiling, and the walls, and the curtains, and the door, Mama hides the paints in the top of the closet. That doesn't stop the baby! After crawling to the top of the closet and retrieving the paints, the baby starts painting his body, beginning with his head. (He paints it red.) The painting continues along with lots of smiles and an even bigger mess.

Predicting/Anticipating

Have students guess what body part the baby will paint next by listening to the rhyming words. Here are some examples:

★ "So take some red and paint my _____." (head)

★ "Aw, what the heck! Gonna paint my _____." (neck)

★ "Still, I just can't rest till I paint my _____." (chest)

Summarizing

This text lends itself well to a retelling.

Story Structure

★ **Characters**—Mama, the baby, and dog

★ **Setting**—The baby's house

★ **Plot**—The baby tends to paint things that his mother would prefer not to be painted, such as the inside of her house and himself.

★ **Resolution**—The baby runs out of paint.

Sequencing

★ Mama puts the paints in the closet.

★ The baby gets the paints.

★ He paints his head.

★ He paints his neck.

★ He paints his chest.

★ He paints his arm.

★ He paints his hand.

★ He paints his back.

★ He paints his leg.

★ He paints his feet.

★ He runs out of paint.

★ He takes a bath.

Karen Kaufman Orloff (G. P. Putnam's Sons, 2004)
0-399-23717-8

Mikey Gulligan is moving and must find a home for his pet iguana. Alex would like to be the new owner of the iguana but first he must convince his mother. He writes his mother persuasive letters giving all of the reasons why he thinks he should be the owner of such a wonderful pet. His mother in return responds to each of Alex's letters with her own reasons why she thinks it is not such a good idea.

The illustrations and Alex's reasoning and obvious deep desire for the pet make this a very entertaining book.

Connecting
★ **Text to Self**—Ask students, "Have you ever tried talking someone into letting you have a pet?"
★ **Text to Text**—*101 Facts About Iguanas* by Sarah Williams (Gareth Stevens Publishing, 2001)
★ **Text to World**—Where might you find iguanas in their natural habitats?

Point of View
Throughout the story, Alex shares several reasons why he thinks he should have an iguana. On the other hand, his mother shares just as many reasons why she thinks he should not have an iguana.

Here are a few of Alex's reasons:
★ If he doesn't take the iguana, Mikey's dog will eat it.
★ They are really quiet and cute.
★ He is so small his mom will never know he's there.
★ He could teach him tricks.

Here are a few of Mom's reasons:
★ Mikey's iguana is uglier than Godzilla.
★ Iguanas can grow to be over six feet long.
★ How will Mikey get a girl to marry him when he owns a six-foot-long reptile?
★ There were problems when Mikey took home the class fish.

Sue Williams (Voyager Books, 1992)
ISBN 0-152-38011-6

This is a cumulative story of a little boy's walk during which he encounters a menagerie of colorful animals—a black cat, a brown horse, a red cow, a green duck, a pink pig, and a yellow dog. By the end of his walk, he has lots of animals following him.

This could be a helpful resource for instruction in colors or in a unit of study about farm animals.

Connecting

★ **Text to Text**—*Brown Bear, Brown Bear, What Do You See?* by Bill Martin, Jr. (Holt, Rinehart, and Winston, 1967)

★ **Text to World**—Many children have seen or read about farm animals.

Predicting/Anticipating

What animal will he see next? Each spread provides a clue to the animal that the boy will encounter next.

Picture Clues

Each spread gives a clue about which animal is coming next.

Ira Sleeps Over

Bernard Waber (Houghton Mifflin Company, 1975)
ISBN 0-395-20503-4

Ira is very excited about the prospect of his first sleepover at Reggie's house. His older sister asks him if he is taking his teddy bear. Now he is concerned about being teased if he takes the bear, or not being able to sleep if he doesn't take it. Reggie has great plans for the evening and they include telling ghost stories. When the story gets scary, Reggie pulls out his teddy bear. Ira decides to go home and get his bear.

Connecting

Text to Self—Many children have stuffed animals that they love.

Summarizing

This text lends itself well to a retelling.

Story Structure

★ **Characters**—Ira, Ira's parents, Ira's sister, Reggie, Reggie's father, Tah Tah, Foo Foo
★ **Setting**—Ira's house, Reggie's house
★ **Plot**—A young boy is excited about his first sleepover, but he is worried about taking his teddy bear along. He decides to go without his bear, but then a scary story makes him want his bear.
★ **Resolution**—Ira returns home to get his bear when Reggie reveals that he also sleeps with his teddy bear.

Problem/Solution

Problem—Ira is unsure about whether he should take his teddy bear to the sleepover.
Solution—After Reggie got out his teddy bear, Ira went back home to get his.

Sequencing

★ Ira plans a sleepover at his neighbor's house.
★ His sister questions him about taking his teddy bear to the sleepover.
★ He goes to the sleepover without the teddy bear.
★ Ira and Reggie play together until Reggie's father calls bedtime.
★ Reggie begins to tell a scary ghost story.
★ Reggie gets out his teddy bear.
★ Ira goes home to get his teddy bear.
★ Ira returns to Reggie's house and finds Reggie already asleep.

Tana Hoban (HarperTrophy, 1997)
ISBN 0-688-15287-2

In this wordless book, Tana Hoban has taken photographs comparing the sizes of objects, animals, and people. Readers and non-readers alike can enjoy the visual concept of compare and contrast with everyday items.

Compare/Contrast

Each page has a visual compare/contrast. Ask students to share the similarities and differences they see. Here are a few of the items:

★ leaves
★ a mother pig and her babies
★ a mixing bowl and measuring cups
★ books
★ beads
★ ears
★ dolls
★ icicles
★ instruments
★ toothbrushes

Picture Clues

This wordless book allows students to make comparisons by using picture clues only.

Helen Lester (Houghton Mifflin Company, 1989)
ISBN 0-395-51007-4

Things just seem to happen to Murdley Gurdson, like falling into wastebaskets and breaking things. But the day he went walking in his one too-big shoe and an egg fell on his head, he was totally an innocent bystander. As he goes from one animal to another trying to find out who is responsible, he discovers that is very difficult to find anyone to take the blame. Finally, he meets a rabbit who says it is his fault. As he was hopping along, he landed in a shoe and became stuck and that was what began the cycle of events that eventually scared the bird and caused it to lay the egg on Murdley's head. After hearing the story, Murdley looks at the familiar shoe and knows that it was all his fault. Afterwards, he and his new friends go back to his house and have a wonderful meal of scrambled eggs.

Connecting

Text to Self—Ask students, "Have you ever felt something wasn't your fault and then found out later that you were responsible? How did you feel?"

Predicting/Anticipating

Who do you think is responsible for Murdley's unfortunate situation?

Story Structure

★ **Characters**—Murdley Gurdson, bird, aardvark, pygmy hippo, rabbit
★ **Setting**—Outside of Murdley's house and inside Murdley's house
★ **Plot**—Murdley Gurdson is trying to figure out who is responsible for an egg landing on his head and everyone has a reason for why it wasn't his fault.
★ **Resolution**—Murdley finally realizes that it was his own fault. When he carelessly left his shoe out, a rabbit accidentally hopped into it and began the series of events that ended with an egg cracking on Murdley's head. He and his friends go back to his house and enjoy a meal of scrambled eggs.

Cause/Effect

This text is very supportive of cause/effect. Here are a few examples:
★ **Cause**—An aardvark screams. **Effect**—The scared bird lays an egg.
★ **Cause**—A pygmy hippo steps on the aardvark's tail. **Effect**—The aardvark screams.
★ **Cause**—A hopping shoe with long ears comes towards the pygmy hippo. **Effect**—As the pygmy hippo tries to get out of the way, he steps on the aardvark's tail.
★ **Cause**—Murdley Gurdson leaves a shoe outside. **Effect**—A rabbit accidentally hops into the shoe.

David Miller (Dial Books for Young Readers, 2001) ISBN 0-803-72586-8

In the majority of this book, comparisons are drawn between animal behavior and human behavior. People and animals are alike in many ways. The last page spread gives information about the animals featured in the book.

Expository Structure

★ The text is in paragraph format.

★ Bold print is used for important words.

★ The text is accompanied by illustrations.

★ Last page spread has information about the animals in the book.

Main Idea/Details

Main Idea—Sometimes animal behavior and human behavior is similar.

Details

★ The bird of paradise shows off.

★ The cheetah moves like the wind.

★ Penguins like to play together.

★ Chameleons try to blend in.

★ Lions lounge lazily.

★ Cranes love to dance.

★ Baby birds are protected by their parents.

Figurative Language

★ **Simile**

• "The golden cheetah moves like the wind."

• "Light as drifting smoke, graceful cranes love to dance."

★ **Alliteration**—"On a summer afternoon, the noble lion lounges lazily."

CD-104192 Using Children's Literature to Enhance Reading Instruction

Dugald Steer (Dutton Children's Books, 1999)
ISBN 0-525-46215-5

It is time for little pig and his sister to go to bed but before they do, he begs Mother Pig for just one more story. He loves listening to stories! After each story Mother Pig reads, he always begs for just one more. After reading the last book, Mother Pig finally gets the result she is hoping for—two little sleeping pigs.

This book is unique because of the four mini-books bound inside. Each of these special books is a retelling of a favorite fairy tale with a piggy twist. You will enjoy *The Pig Prince*, *The Ugly Pigling*, *Piggerella*, and *The Prince and the Porker*.

Connecting

Text to Text

This one book allows for connections to multiple stories.

★ *The Pig Prince—The Frog Prince* adapted by Jon Scieszka from the Brothers Grimm (Penguin Putnam Books for Young Readers, 1994)

★ *The Ugly Pigling—The Ugly Duckling* by Hans Christian Anderson (William Morrow & Company, 1999)

★ *Piggerella—Cinderella* by Charles Perrault (Seastar Books, 2000)

★ *The Prince and the Porker—The Prince and the Pauper* by Mark Twain (Tor Books, 1992)

★ *Time for a Tale* by Dugald Steer (Penguin Putnam Books for Young Readers,, 2002)

Story Structure

★ **Characters**—Mother Pig, the little pig, and the little pig's sister

★ **Setting**—Little pig's home

★ **Plot**—Little pig begs his mother to continue reading just one more story before bedtime.

★ **Resolution**—Mother Pig reads until finally, after the fourth story, both little pigs fall fast asleep.

Compare/Contrast

When you are teaching compare/contrast with text-to-text connections, you have four excellent examples in one book. Here are some compare/contrast examples for *The Ugly Pigling* and *The Ugly Duckling*:

★ **Similarities**
  • The mother is a duck.
  • The mother duck has four fluffy, gorgeous yellow ducklings.
  • The fifth "duckling" doesn't fit in.
  • The fifth "duckling" isn't treated fairly by the other characters.

★ **Differences**

- In *The Ugly Pigling,* the fifth "duckling" is a pig, not a swan.
- In *The Ugly Pigling,* the other animals thought he was a turkey
- During the quacking lesson in *The Ugly Pigling,* the fifth "duckling" says, "OINK."
- In *The Ugly Pigling,* when they figured out that he was a pig, they drove him away.
- The ugly pigling found his way to a farm where the other pigs thought he was handsome.

Diane deGroat (SeaStar Books, 2003)
ISBN 1-587-17214-3

Gilbert and his friends are performing plays for their class. He is assigned to a group with Phillip and Margaret. Each of them chooses a slip of paper to find out which part they will play. Gilbert has the part of George Washington. He practices his lines all day long. He is so excited about his part that, even though he isn't supposed to, he takes home the hat he is supposed to wear in the play so that he can practice. In addition to practicing his lines for the play, Gilbert also practices telling the truth. By telling the truth, he manages to hurt his mother's feelings and makes Lola cry. He puts the hat back into his backpack so he can take it to school the next

day. When it is time to get ready for the play, Gilbert goes to his backpack to get the hat, but it isn't there. Gilbert lets Phillip take the blame for having taken the hat home. When his mother brings the hat to school, Gilbert apologizes for letting Phillip take the blame and goes on to do a good job with his part in the play.

Connecting
Text to Text—*The Honest-to-Goodness Truth* by Patricia C. McKissack (Aladdin, 2003)

Summarizing
This text lends itself well to a retelling.

Story Structure
★ **Characters**—Gilbert, Mrs. Byrd, Phillip, Margaret, classmates, Mother, Lola
★ **Setting**—school, Gilbert's house
★ **Plot**—Gilbert is playing the part of George Washington in the class play. He finds out that telling the truth is important, not only in the play, but in life.
★ **Resolution**—Gilbert tells the truth about taking home the hat and apologizes to his friends.

Picture Clues
When Gilbert is in the bathtub rehearsing his lines for the play, the illustration shows his sister playing with the hat. This explains why it is not in his backpack the next day.

Theme (stated)
Honesty

Paul Showers (HarperTrophy, 1993)
ISBN 0-064-43322-6

A little girl goes for a walk with her father and their dog, Major. Major is old and walks slowly. On this walk, they do not talk. Her father thinks, the dog sniffs, and she listens. They walk on the sidewalk past lawns, on busy streets, and in the park. She becomes aware of all sorts of sounds in her world, and she gives her imitation of those sounds.

Connecting

★ **Text to Self**—Many children have gone on walks with adults that are special to them.

★ **Text to World**—Some readers will have heard sounds like those mentioned by the little girl.

Applying

At the end of the book, the reader is invited to close the book and listen.

Figurative Language

★ **Simile**—"The woodpecker sounds like a little hammer."

★ **Onomatopoeia**—Each page gives examples of the sounds the little girl encounters during her walk. Here are some examples:

- Major's toenails—twick, twick
- Father's shoes—dop, dup
- Lawn mower—z-z-z-z-z-zzzzzzooooooooooooommmmmm
- Sprinklers—whithhh, whithhh

Margaret Wise Brown (HarperTrophy, 2005)
ISBN 0-060-77891-1

Little scarecrow boy lives with his scarecrow parents in a cornfield where the scarecrow father guards the corn. Little scarecrow boy wants to help his father in the cornfields, but his father tells him that he is not yet fierce enough. Scarecrow boy practices his six terrible faces every day. Then, one day, he decides to go into the fields alone, before his parents get up. A big black crow comes into the field, and little scarecrow boy tries five of his scary faces, but still the crow keeps coming. Finally, he tries his last scary face. The crow flies backward. Scarecrow boy thinks he is the fiercest scarecrow in all the fields. Then, he sees his father's shadow.

Predicting/Anticipating
What will happen to scarecrow boy when he goes to the field alone?

Summarizing
This text lends itself well to a retelling.

Inferring
Why did the crow fly off? Scarecrow boy's father was behind him and frightened the crow.

Story Structure
★ **Characters**—scarecrow, scarecrow wife, scarecrow boy, crows
★ **Setting**—scarecrow house, cornfield
★ **Plot**—A little scarecrow boy wants to help his father scare away the crows, but his father keeps telling him that he is not yet fierce enough. Early one morning, the little scarecrow boy goes out alone to the field. A big crow comes flying at him, so the scarecrow boy tries all of his scary faces to frighten the crow off.
★ **Resolution**—Scarecrow boy's father stands behind the scarecrow boy and frightens away the crow.

A Log's Life

Wendy Pfeffer (Simon & Schuster Children's Publishing, 1997)
ISBN 0-689-80636-1

The life cycle of a tree is the subject of this book. A great oak tree stands in the forest. In its trunk and branches live many animals that weaken the tree. A strong wind blows and the mighty oak crashes to the ground. Now, the mighty tree is a log. Many animals create their habitats in and around the log on the forest floor. The activities of the animals living in the log cause it to decompose and form a welcoming environment for new life. An acorn falls into the spot where the log was. The acorn sprouts and grows until a great oak tree again stands in this place in the forest.

Beautiful three-dimensional paper sculptures illustrate the forest ecosystem.

Cause/Effect

Cause—The many activities of the animals living in the tree weaken it so that it becomes vulnerable. **Effect**—The strong winds, rain, and lightning of a storm send the tree crashing to the forest floor.

Main Idea/Details

★ **Main Idea**—The great oak tree provides food and shelter for many animals.
   Details
- Squirrels live in a hole in the tree's trunk.
- Porcupines chew on its branches.
- A colony of ants nests under the bark.
- A woodpecker searches in the bark for insects to eat.
- Beetles burrow under the bark.
- Slugs and snails crawl into the trunk.

★ **Main Idea**—There are forces that cause the tree to decompose and become the earth that will support the acorn that will sprout into a new tree.
   Details
- A spider finds a dry spot for her egg sac.
- Millipedes live between the log and the wet ground.
- Termites move in and eat the rotting log and lay their eggs.
- A porcupine moves into the log.
- Click beetles and salamanders move into the log.
- Bugs and slugs crawl inside the log.

Author's Purpose

To inform

Charles R. Smith, Jr. (Dutton Juvenile, 2001)
ISBN 0-525-46700-9

Loki and Alex are best friends. Loki is Alex's dog, and Alex is Loki's boy. This book is a photographic journey through one of their play sessions seen from both of their points of view.

Author's Purpose

★ To inform the reader about some of the differences between humans and dogs

★ To entertain the reader with engaging text and photographs

Point of View

Each spread shows an event from Loki and Alex's playtime from each character's perspective. This is reinforced through the black and white photographs from Loki's point of view and the color photographs from Alex's point of view.

Theme

The author shows that humans and pets don't always think alike, but want the same things—love and attention.

Jeanne Modesitt (Aladdin, 1999)
ISBN 0-689-82412-2

Little Bunny is wondering whether his mother would like for him to be different. Would she wish that he never cried, got scared, got mad, made mistakes, or looked differently? Mama Rabbit is quick to let him know that she will love him no matter what. She has only one wish for her little bunny. She only wants him to be himself, because she loves him just the way he is.

Connecting

Text to Self—Everybody has times when they are insecure.

Predicting/Anticipating

After each of Little Bunny's questions, readers should be thinking ahead to Mama Rabbit's response. Readers should anticipate what Mama Rabbit's response will be to Little Bunny's question regarding what wish she would make for him.

Summarizing

This text lends itself well to a retelling.

Theme (Implied)

People (children) should be happy with themselves just as they are.

Mike and the Bike

Michael Ward (Cookie Jar Publishing, 2005)
ISBN 1-59441-498-X

Enjoy this tale about Mike and the thing he loves most—his wonderful bike. He shares their travel adventures and the world they discover together. His technique of riding and the special care he takes with his bike are described in a toe-tapping rhyming verse. An audio CD with a cycle bell that rings when it is time to turn the page is included. At the completion of the recorded reading, the CD includes several songs. The lyrics are printed in the back of the book. An extra added bonus is a foreword by Lance Armstrong and colorful biking photographs at the end of the book.

Connecting

★ **Text to Self**—Ask students, "Do you enjoy riding your bike and wearing a helmet like Mike? How do you take care of your bike? Have you ever been in a bike race?"

★ **Text to World**—Have you ever watched bike races? What do you know about Lance Armstrong?

Applying

Ask students, "Is biking something you would like to do? Do you wear a helmet each time you ride your bike?"

Missing: One Stuffed Rabbit

Maryann Cocca-Leffler (Albert Whitman & Company, 2000)
ISBN 0-807-55162-7

Every Friday, someone in Mrs. Robin's second-grade class gets to take home the class's stuffed toy rabbit, Coco. Coco travels with his diary. Each student helps Coco record his thoughts from his visit. One Friday, it is Janine's turn. She takes Coco to visit her Nana. On Saturday, they do everything together. On Sunday, the family goes shopping, and, somehow, Janine loses Coco in the shopping mall. The whole class tries to help find Coco. They make posters and hang them at the mall. They discover that Coco has been given to the local hospital through a toy distribution program. As it turns out, Coco has been given to a little girl with a broken leg who needs him much more than the class does. Coco stays with the little girl, Teresa. The whole class writes to Coco and Teresa.

Connecting

★ **Text to Self**—Most readers have lost something that is really important to them.
★ **Text to Text**—*Felix Travels Back in Time* by Annette Langen (Parklane Publishing, 2004)
★ **Text to World**—Some students may have gotten separated from their parents at a mall.

Summarizing

This text lends itself well to a retelling.

Applying

This text gives a great year-long project idea to students and their teachers. They can also have a stuffed animal that travels with members of the class. Students can write in a diary each day about the adventures they have when the stuffed animal goes home with them.

Story structure

★ **Characters**—Coco, Janine, Mrs. Robin, classmates, Teresa
★ **Setting**—classroom, mall, hospital
★ **Plot**—Janine gets to take Coco home for the weekend. She loses Coco in the mall. The students in the class work together to find Coco.
★ **Resolution**—Coco goes to live with Teresa.

Problem/Solution

★ **Problem**—Coco is lost.
★ **Solution**—The class discovers a toy distribution center at the mall and finds that Coco has been given to a little girl.

Theme (Implied)

Responsibility and self-sacrifice

CD-104192 ★ Using Children's Literature to Enhance Reading Instruction

Tedd Arnold (Puffin, 2003)
ISBN 0-142-50149-2

A little boy is very concerned about the phrases he hears in the everyday language of the people in his life. He is taking the comments they are making to him literally. He is becoming afraid that his body will fly apart.

This hilarious rhyming book is full of idioms that are commonly used in everyday speech. Delightful illustrations add to the fun.

Figurative language
Idioms

★ "I'll bet that broke your heart."
★ "Like when my dad asked me if I would please give him a hand."
★ "It's sure to crack you up."
★ "She said to stretch our arms and legs . . . ."
★ "Hold your tongue . . . ."
★ "He gets so nervous that he nearly jumps out of his skin."
★ "He claims his baby sister screams her lungs out every night."
★ "We thought you'd lost your mind."

George Shannon (Greenwillow, 2001)
ISBN 0-688-17643-7

This book is filled with 18 folktales from around the world. Each story requires the reader to use critical thinking skills to decide which part of the story the character has chosen to tell the whole truth and which part he or she has chosen to misrepresent. The students enjoy the challenge of trying to figure out the whole truth before turning to the answer page.

Connecting

Text to World—The stories in this book are from all over the world. Background information about each story and where it originated is on pages 63 and 64.

Concluding

Each of the stories ends with the reader needing to decide what is the truth and what is the lie. Here is a synopsis of one story:

A man in Trinidad has been arrested. When he is asked why he was arrested, he responds by saying he only picked up a rope he had found on the ground. The man is only telling half of the truth and the reader is asked to decide what the man is telling that is true and what the man did not tell that makes him guilty.

The reader turns the page to find someone's cow at the end of the rope.

Gloria Houston (HarperTrophy, 1997)
ISBN 0-064-43374-9

Arizona Houston grew up in the Blue Ridge mountains with her little brother, Jim. They had a rich life full of fun and laughter. When her mother died, Arizona had to leave school to stay home and take care of Papa and Jim. She loved to read and dream about faraway places. When her father remarried, Arizona was able to go away to live with her aunt so that she could go to school where she studied to become a teacher. She returned to her home on Henson Creek where she taught school for 57 years.

This book is a good resource in a study of the Blue Ridge mountain area.

Connecting

Text to Self—Ask students, "Have you played games and participated in other kinds of activities like Arizona and Jim played when they were young?"

Summarizing

This text lends itself well to a retelling.

Imaging

There are several places in the text with descriptions of Arizona. This provides an opportunity to support children with building mental images as they read. Invite students to close their eyes and try to build a mental image of Arizona's appearance based on the description the author gives.

Compare/Contrast

How is life in the reader's area similar or different from Arizona's life in the Blue Ridge mountains? Listed below are some of the similarities and differences.

★ **Similarities**
- Children usually like to play with their siblings.
- Children go to school.
- Students eat lunch.
- Students play at recess.

★ Differences
- Arizona and Jim climbed in the mountains.
- They made snow cream and maple-sugar candy.
- The school was called a blab school.
- Students carried their lunches in tin buckets.
- When Arizona became a teacher, she carried her baby to school with her.

Character Analysis
Arizona has a very strong work ethic. She leaves school at a young age to take care of Papa and Jim. She works hard for Aunt Suzie and to get the education she needs to be a teacher. She teaches school for 57 years.

Theme (Implied)
The value in reading many books

My Teacher Sleeps in School

Leatie Weiss (Puffin, 1985)
ISBN 0-140-50559-8

The students in Mrs. Marsh's class have decided that she sleeps at school and are looking for clues to prove their theory. They found a towel, soap, and a mirror in the closet and a bag with paper plates, napkins, forks, and spoons. Their final discovery of slippers and a pillow under her desk make believers out of the entire class. What they are not ready for is the field trip that Mrs. Marsh has planned for them when she takes them to her real house for a surprise party with cake and decorations.

Connecting

Text to Self—Ask students, "Have you ever wondered where your teacher lives?"

Concluding

Throughout the text, the students are looking for clues that will help them draw a conclusion as to whether or not Mrs. Marsh really does sleep in school. A few of the clues that help them reach that conclusion are:

★ She was there when they arrived and when they left.

★ They found a towel, soap, and a mirror.

★ They found paper plates, napkins, forks, spoons, a cake mix, and eggs.

★ They found a pair of slippers and a pillow under her desk.

Imaging

The students in the book visualized Mrs. Marsh living at school. Have your students close their eyes and try to see the following images in their minds. In the book, they thought of her getting dressed and undressed in the closet, putting gloppy cream on her face, wearing funny pajamas, eating supper in their play kitchen area, doing her laundry, brushing her teeth, and sleeping in different areas of the room.

Karma Wilson (Little, Brown and Company, 2004)
ISBN 0-316-98564-3

One little shout in the zoo from a young girl who has dropped her ice cream cone starts a chain reaction. It begins with a frightened bear who charges by a moose who trots by an ape who steals the zookeeper's keys and lets out all of the animals. This cumulative tale ends with all of the people in the zoo being locked up by the animals.

Connecting

Text to Text—*If You Give a Mouse a Cookie* (HarperCollins Children's Books, 1985) and other Laura Numeroff books (HarperCollins Children's Books).

Predicting/Anticipating

What will happen next after each event?

Cause/Effect

- ★ **Cause**—The little girl shouts. **Effect**—A bear is frightened and charges.
- ★ **Cause**—A moose sees the bear is free. **Effect**—The moose wants to be free.
- ★ **Cause**—The moose escapes and trots by the apes. **Effect**—The apes come up with a plan.
- ★ **Cause**—The apes steal the keys. **Effect**—All of the animals are freed.

Picture Clues

The illustrations begin to tell this story before the actual text begins. Observe the illustrations on the Title, Copyright, and Dedication pages to find out why the little girl feels the need to shout in the zoo.

Mem Fox (Voyager Books, 1992)
ISBN 0-152-57421-2

Miss Lily Laceby is snug in her cottage with her dog, Butch Aggie. As Lily snoozes in her easy chair, there are noises going on all around and even though Butch Aggie hears them, Lily sleeps on, dreaming her dreams. There are sounds of car doors opening and closing, feet tiptoeing, voices murmuring, door knobs attempting to turn, and knuckles knocking. Through it all, Lily keeps dreaming until she hears the knocking on her door, voices shouting at the windows, and Butch Aggie's barking. When Lily gets to the door, she finds her family there to surprise her for her 90th birthday.

Predicting/Anticipating

After reading the first few pages, have students predict who they think is outside Lily's cottage.

Inferring

★ Ask students, "Who is Lily dreaming about?"

★ Ask students, "How does Butch Aggie feel about Lily?"

★ After reading the book, ask students, "How old do you think Lily really is?"

Sequencing

This book allows for four different sequencing opportunities. Select either the people sneaking up to Lily's cottage, Butch Aggie's different responses to the noises, Lily's dreams, or the entire story line. Below is an example of sequencing Lily's dreams using the picture clues:

★ A woman is caring for a gentleman.

★ A couple is holding a newborn baby.

★ A couple is together on their wedding day.

★ A girl is riding a horse.

★ A young girl is going to school.

★ A little girl is swinging.

Figurative Language
★ **Simile**

• Her hair was as wispy as cobwebs in ceilings.

• Her bones were as creaky as floorboards at midnight.

★ **Personification**—"Outside, clouds raced along the sky, playing hide-and seek with the moon."

★ **Onomatopoeia**
  - "CLICK. CLACK."
  - "CRINCH. CRUNCH."
  - "MURMUR, MUTTER, SHHHH"
  - "RATTLE"
  - "KNICK, KNACK, KNOCK"
  - "YELL, CLATTER, BANG, BANG"
  - "CREAK, CRACK"
  - "SNICK, SNACK"

Picture Clues

This is a very strong book for teaching the importance of picture clues. The majority of the book consists of pages with three different scenes that are taking place at the same time. The pages give readers a visual of what is going on outside of Lily's cottage, Lily sitting in her chair sleeping while her dog reacts to the different noises outside, and the images from Lily's dream. Here are some examples of how the illustrations reveal the author's intentions:

Pages 5 and 6
The first illustration reveals car doors opening.
The second illustration shows Lily sleeping in her chair as Butch Aggie listens.
The third illustration allows readers to see into her dreams where a woman is caring for a sick gentleman.

Pages 7 and 8
The first illustration reveals feet tiptoeing up the garden path.
The second illustration shows Lily still sleeping and Butch Aggie listening to the new noises.
The third illustration has Lily dreaming about a couple holding a newborn baby.

Pages 8 and 9
The first illustration reveals voices whispering in the bushes.
The second illustration shows Lily still dreaming in her chair and Butch Aggie bristling.
The third illustration has Lily dreaming of a couple on their wedding day.

Eve Bunting (Voyager Books, 1994)
ISBN 0-152-00121-2

On Christmas Eve, the narrator of the story and his family go to Luke's Forest for their annual event, to decorate their Christmas tree. They take a red lantern, blanket, decorations of food for the animals, and hot chocolate. They enjoy their evening by decorating the tree, singing songs and observing the animals. Later, at bedtime and during the next day, the narrator imagines the animals in Luke's Forest celebrating different Christmas activities.

Connecting

Text to Self—This book allows for great discussions about holiday traditions.

Predicting

Ask students, "After reading the first eight pages, what do you think the family might be planning to do? After reading page nine, could you add to your prediction? Read page 14 and see if you would like to change or add to your prediction."

Imaging/Inferring

★ **Imaging**

The text has several different areas that are good for imaging. Ask students to specify which sense you would use when reading the following text:

- "We drive through the bright Christmas streets to where the dark and quiet begin."
- ". . . rolls down the windows so we can smell the tree smell."
- "I . . . toast my hands around my warm cup."
- "It has been our tree forever and ever. We walk around it, touching it."
- "It's so cold my breath hurts."
- "A deer is watching us. I see the brightness of its eyes . . . ."
- "An owl hoots, deep in the darkness."
- "Our tree looks so pretty."
- "Before we leave she and I get to choose a Christmas carol to sing."

★ **Inferring**

After reading the following text, how would you describe Nina?

- "'It's grown since last year,' I say. Mom puts her hand on my shoulder. 'So have you.' 'So have I,' Nina says. Nina hates to be left out."

- "Can I put on the popcorn chain?" Nina asks. She hops up and down and right out of one of her boots. Mom helps her get it back on.

What do you think the narrator might mean in this statement?

- "An owl hoots, deep in the darkness. There are secrets all around us."

Rick Walton (Putnam Juvenile, 1998)
ISBN 0-698-11607-0

The bullfrog has lost his hop. He searches for his hop in all sorts of places—under a toad . . . stool, behind a dog . . . house, and under a hedge . . . hog. Finally, he encounters a diamondback rattlesnake looking for breakfast. He remembers how to hop when the snake tries to eat him.

Compound words are split over two page spreads, inviting the reader to predict the second part of the compound word.

Predicting/Anticipating
What will be the second part of each compound word?

Summarizing
This text lends itself well to a retelling.

Problem/Solution
★ **Problem**—Bullfrog has lost his hop.
★ **Solution**—He finds it when he is about to become the diamondback rattlesnake's breakfast. He leaps into the air higher than the sun.

Picture Clues
Each two-page spread has an illustration which will either assist the reader or give the reader a false impression of what the second part of the compound word will be.

Colin McNaughton (Voyager Books, 2000)
ISBN 0-152-02458-1

Mr. Wolf is hungry, and he has his eyes on Preston Pig. Preston Pig is a bit of a klutz and is making a mess at home. His mother sends him to take a basket of food to his sick Granny. Preston's Mom reminds him to put on his coat, which happens to be a red cape with a hood. Mr. Wolf follows him through the woods to Granny's house. He tries several tricks to catch Preston Pig in the woods, but they all fail. This reminds Mr. Wolf of another story, but he can't remember which one. He makes it to Granny's house and hears Granny and Preston talking. When Granny uses some of Mr. Wolf's lines from *Little Red Riding Hood*, Mr. Wolf remembers the story, but he still can't remember how it ends. He ties Granny up and stuffs Preston in a sack. Suddenly, when Preston Pig's dad, a woodcutter, arrives, Mr. Wolf remembers the ending.

Connecting
Text to Text
★ *Little Red Riding Hood* by The Brothers Grimm (Penguin Putnam Books for Young Readers, 1991)
★ *The Wolf's Story* by Brenda Parkes (Rigby, 2000)

Summarizing
This text lends itself well to a retelling.

Point of View
Mr. Wolf tells parts of fairy tales the way his mother had told him.

Ordinary Mary's Extraordinary Deed

Emily Pearson (Gibbs Smith, 2002)
ISBN 0-879-05978-8

This story is about a little girl named Mary who touched the entire world by just doing one kind deed. Mary's deed was as simple as picking a bowl of blueberries and leaving them on Mrs. Bishop's porch. Mrs. Bishop made muffins from the berries and secretly gave them to five people that she thought might have left them for her. Each of these five in return did a kind deed for five more people with the cycle continuing and in 15 days over six billion people had shared a kind deed all because of one ordinary little girl named Mary.

This is a great book to pass on!

Connecting
★ **Text to Self**—Ask students, "What are some kind deeds that you have done? What are some kind deeds that everyone can do?"
★ **Text to Text**—*One Smile* by Cindy McKinley (Illumination Arts Publishing, Inc., 2002)
★ **Text to World**—Ask students, "What are some things that people might do to help this be a better or safer place to live?"

Applying
Discuss with students how they might attempt to do a daily kind deed for someone and possibly keep it a secret as Mary did. At the end of the day, you might ask if anyone did a kind deed. Be sure to call attention to kind deeds you observe during the day.

Cause/Effect
Mary begins the cause/effect cycle and it continues throughout the book. Here are a few examples:
★ **Cause**—Mary gives Mrs. Bishop blueberries. **Effect**—Mrs. Bishop makes blueberry muffins.
★ **Cause**—Mrs. Bishop gives Billy the paperboy some muffins. **Effect**—Billy is so glad that he hands newspapers to the next five people on his route instead of throwing them in the bushes.
★ **Cause**—Mrs. Bishop gives Mr. Stevens blueberry muffins. **Effect**—He smiles on the airplane for 10 hours and offers to help five different people with their bags.

Our Granny

Margaret Wild (Houghton Mifflin Company, 1998)
0-395-88395-4

Two small children share their background knowledge about grannies and what makes their grannies unique. In a few words, they will take you from laughter to tears.

Julie Vivas's watercolor illustrations are beautiful and on certain pages bring a giggle from the students. This is a book to enjoy!

Connecting

Text to Self—Ask students, "Do you have a granny and does she fit into any of these categories?"

Main Idea/Details

The main idea of the book is grannies. Throughout the book are details describing where grannies live, what they have, what they wear, what they do, how they play, and how they give you kisses.

★ **Main Idea**—Where do grannies live?
Details
- Apartments
- Big old houses
- Old people's homes
- Little rooms in the city
- Trailers
- Farmhouses
- Cottages by the ocean
- Nursing homes
- Nowhere at all
- With their families

★ **Main Idea**—What do grannies have?
Details
- Thin legs
- Fat knees
- Bristly chins
- Interesting hair
- Crinkly eyes
- Friendly smiles
- Big soft laps
- Wobbly bottoms

★ **Main Idea**—What do grannies wear?
Details
- Jeans and sneakers
- Pantsuits
- Silky dresses
- Big bras
- Baggy underwear
- Lots of jewelry
- High heels
- Sensible shoes
- Comfy slippers
- Funny bathing suits

★ ★ ★ ★ CD-104192 ★ Using Children's Literature to Enhance Reading Instruction

The Pain and the Great One

Judy Blume (Dragonfly Books, 1985)
ISBN 0-440-40967-5

A six-year-old boy and his eight-year-old sister see each other as the best loved by their parents. Each thinks the other is a troublemaker and is being doted on and indulged. The first part of the book is the sister's story of how she sees her younger brother, The Pain. She is upset about many things—he won't get out of bed, mom carries him into the kitchen, and dad helps him get dressed. Her parents say that The Pain is just what they always wanted. She thinks they love him the best. The second part of the book is the brother's story of how he sees his older sister, The Great One. He is upset about many things—daddy and mom think she's really smart, she can play the piano and her songs are recognizable, she can work the can opener, and she can remember phone numbers. His parents say that  The Great One is just what they always wanted. He thinks they love her the best.

Connecting
Text to Self—Many children have siblings of whom they are jealous.

Summarizing
This text lends itself well to a retelling.

Compare/Contrast
Life for this six-year-old and eight-year-old has some similarities and differences.
★ Similarities
  • They eat breakfast at the table.
  • They go to school.
  • They ride the bus to school.
  • They show their homework to their mom.
  • They have dessert after dinner.
  • They go to bed at the same time.
  • Their parents love them equally.

★ **Differences**

- Mom carries The Pain to the breakfast table.
- Dad helps The Pain get dressed.
- The Pain gets to show his homework to mom first.
- The Pain gets dessert even if he doesn't eat his dinner.
- The Pain messes up the bathroom.
- The cat sleeps on The Pain's bed.
- The Great One feeds the cat.
- The Great One plays the piano well.
- The Great One can work the can opener.
- The Great One is old enough to hold their aunt's baby.
- The Great One can remember phone numbers.
- The Great One and her friends can build cities with blocks.
- The Great One can swim and dive.
- The Pain is afraid to put his face in the water.

Point of View

Ordinary incidents in the lives of The Pain and The Great One are recounted from their own perspectives. They see these situations from entirely different vantage points.

The Paperboy

Dav Pilkey (Orchard Books, 1999)
ISBN 0-531-07139-1

A boy and his dog get up before the rest of the family, while it is still dark, and deliver newspapers. It's hard for him and his dog to leave the warm bed and go out into the cold of the early morning. The boy and his dog quietly go downstairs without waking his mom, dad, and sister. They eat breakfast from their bowls, and then they go about their tasks of folding the newspapers, snapping on rubber bands, placing the bound papers in a bag, and then delivering them. They know the route by heart. The world wakes up around them as they head back home with their empty bag. When the rest of the family wakes up, they head back to bed.

This text would be one good resource for an author study showing the different writing styles of Dav Pilkey. The style in *The Paperboy* can be compared with his humorous writing in the *Captain Underpants* series (Scholastic, Inc.) or *'Twas the Night Before Thanksgiving* (Scholastic Paperbacks, 2004).

Summarizing
This text lends itself well to a retelling.

Imaging
This text invites the reader to create mental images of the early morning and how things change as the world begins to wake up. The stars and moon fade and the sky begins to change colors. Invite students to close their eyes and try to build mental images of the morning sky as it begins to change color.

Applying
When people do a good job with their responsibilities, they rest well.

Sequencing
★ The paperboy and his dog get up early.
★ They quietly go downstairs.
★ They eat breakfast.

- ★ They get the papers ready for delivery.
- ★ They deliver the papers.
- ★ The world begins to wake up.
- ★ They race back home.
- ★ The rest of the family is awake.
- ★ The boy and the dog go back to bed.

Character Analysis

This young boy is responsible. He does his job, even though it is hard to get out of bed and face the cold outside. He is considerate. He tries very hard not to disturb the rest of the family as he goes about getting ready for work.

Themes (Implied)

- ★ Satisfaction in a job well done
- ★ Responsibility

A Present for Mom

Vivian French (Candlewick, 2005)
ISBN 0-763-62692-9

Mother's Day is coming and Stanley doesn't have a present for his mother even though each of his siblings does. His big brother is giving her flowers. His big sister is giving her a box of candy. His biggest sister is baking a cake for their mother. He tries to imitate each of their presents but fails abysmally. He can't seem to come up with just the right present for his mother. That night, Stanley doesn't sleep very well. Just in the nick of time, Stanley comes up with the perfect present, a box full of kisses.

Connecting

Text to Self—Many people have had trouble coming up with an idea for a present.

Predicting/Anticipating

★ What is Stanley's idea?
★ What is in Stanley's box?

Summarizing

This text lends itself well to a retelling.

Inferring

Why isn't Stanley able to sleep well?

Evaluating

★ **Criterion for Comparison**—Many people seek to give expensive elaborate gifts.
★ **Evaluation of Text**—The author uses a charming story to help us realize that material presents aren't always the best.

Story Structure

★ **Characters**—Stanley, Flora, Rex, Queenie, Mom
★ **Setting**—Stanley's house and yard
★ **Plot**—Stanley doesn't have a present for Mom. He tries to imitate the presents of his older siblings.
★ **Resolution**—He gives Mom a box of kisses for Mother's Day.

Problem/Solution

★ **Problem**—Stanley doesn't have a present and is having trouble coming up with an original idea.
★ **Solution**—When it is time to give their presents to Mom, Stanley's big sister, Flora, tells him to just give Mom a kiss. Stanley comes up with the idea to give Mom a whole box full of kisses.

Sequencing

★ Stanley asks Rex what he is giving Mom.

★ Stanley picks flowers, but all of the petals fell off.

★ Stanley asks Queenie what she is giving Mom.

★ Stanley has no money to buy candy.

★ Stanley asks Flora what she is giving Mom.

★ Stanley trips and drops his mud cake.

★ Stanley can't sleep well.

★ Flora tells Stanley to give Mom a kiss.

★ Flora, Queenie, and Rex go downstairs to give Mom their presents.

★ Stanley gives Mom a cardboard box.

★ Mom opens the box only to find that it is empty.

★ Stanley tells them all that it is a box of kisses.

Picture Clues

The illustrations give the reader clues about why Stanley isn't sleeping well. There are pictures of flowers, candy, and a cake floating around.

A Quiet Place

Douglas Wood (Aladdin, 2005)
ISBN 0-689-87609-2

Through a little boy's imagination, Douglas Wood shares all of the places a person might go to get away from the noise of the hectic world. As he "travels" to a desert island, forest, beach, desert, pond, cave, hilltop, snowdrift, museum, and a library, he uses details and visual images to paint vivid pictures in the reader's mind. This book invites the reader to find that special, quiet place within for a quiet place.

Imaging

Throughout the book, Wood refers to the sensations the boy might experience during his adventures. Invite students to close their eyes and try to see, hear, or feel what the author is describing. Here are a few examples:

★ **Sound**—Ask students if they can hear sounds in their heads when you read the following words in the text: "bells ringing," "waves roaring," "gulls crying," "footsteps echoing," "the dripping of an icicle," "falling snow whispers," "'S-H-H-H-H.'"

★ **Sight**—Ask students to close their eyes and visualize as you read. Here are some passages that can especially help them draw mental pictures: "Old Man Saguaro reaching for the sky," "thunderheads blooming," "a horn toad blinking," "water that is so calm it looks like a mirror."

★ **Feeling**—Ask students to close their eyes and imagine what the following would feel like: "You are 'reeling in a monster catch,' you feel the cold and dampness of a cave, your legs become too tired for climbing a hill."

Evaluating

★ **Criterion for Comparison**—Most people have times when they need to get away from the frantic pace of everyday life.

★ **Evaluation of Text**—This author gives many examples where an individual can escape and have quiet reflections.

Figurative Language

★ **Simile**

- "The water is so calm it looks like a mirror."
- "New rocks that hang like icicles or stand like sculptures."
- "Where clouds float by like ships or alligators or elephants."

★ **Personification**

- "Wind sings in the leaves."
- "All around you the falling snow whispers, '"S-H-H-H-H"' and wraps the world in silence."
- "If you listen closely, you can almost hear it breathing." (referring to the snow)

★ **Onomatopoeia**

- "Drip, drip"
- "S-h-h-h"

Theme (Implied)

Everyone needs to find their own quiet place to escape from the hectic pace of the world.

CD-104192 Using Children's Literature to Enhance Reading Instruction

Salmon Creek

Annette LeBox and Karen Reczuch (Groundwood Books, 2005)
ISBN 0-888-99644-6

Written in the voice of Sumi the salmon, this story begins when she is still in her egg casing and takes you through her entire life cycle. She shares her thoughts with the reader, as well as what she sees, feels, hears, tastes, and smells. Soon it feels as if the reader is swimming alongside Sumi in the cool creek water.

The beautiful watercolor illustrations by Karen Reczuch and an informational life cycle time line of the salmon are additional reasons for reading the book.

Connecting

Text to World—Exactly what is happening to the endangered salmon and where do they live?

Imaging

There are numerous opportunities for imaging within this text. Ask students to close their eyes and try to see, hear, feel, smell, or taste, what the author is describing. Here are a few examples:

★ **Sight**—". . . darkness so complete she could barely imagine another world larger than the egg case enclosing her."

★ **Sound**—". . . she could hear the wind whispering through the cedars. She could hear the creek stones lifting and falling as the salmon mothers built their nests."

★ **Smell**
  • "Home is the scent of cedar and creek."
  • "The scent of the salmon lingered in the air."
  • "She widened her nostrils, memorized each scent: moss and fern and cedar, maple and damp earth!"

★ **Taste**
  • "As she tasted salt water, her body felt strange."
  • "She feasted on sand lance and candlefish and shrimp-like creatures called krill!"

★ **Feel**—"She rode the currents, her muscles straining, her fins tattered, her strength waning, but she wouldn't stop, she couldn't stop . . ."

Applying

Discuss with students what their roles might be in helping to protect the Pacific Salmon. In the back of the book, there is a page entitled "Threats to Pacific Salmon," which gives ideas about how readers can help. A Web site address is included.

Expository Structure

★ Time line

★ Glossary

★ Information regarding threats, how kids can help, and additional resources

Sequencing

This text lends itself well for sequencing as the reader follows the life cycle of the salmon. Follow up sequencing by looking at the time line in the back of the book.

★ In the late fall, a female salmon lays eggs.

★ The male fertilizes the eggs.

★ Eleven or twelve days later, the female and male die.

★ In December or January, the eggs hatch.

★ In March or April, the young salmon lose their egg sacs and become fry.

★ The fry swim and hunt for food.

★ After a year, in April or May, the salmon are now smolts.

★ The smolts begin to migrate down river.

★ By late June, the smolts should have reached the sea.

★ They are now called coho and they will spend 16 to 18 months in the sea eating and growing.

★ The next summer they begin their journey back home.

★ As they leave the sea and swim back into fresh water (which could take up to six months), their bodies begin to change.

★ When they return to their birthplace, the mother salmon lays the eggs and the cycle continues.

Author's Purpose

★ To inform

★ To entertain

Figurative Language

★ **Simile**

- "She was as small as a pine needle, scared and alone."

- "Then Nulluk showered her eggs with milt, and the water of the creek flowed white, like milk."

★ **Personification**—"Sumi was blind, but she could hear the wind whispering through the cedars."

Context Clues

fry, smolt, estuary, kelp, krill

★ "When her egg sac was empty, she swam upward, followed a school of **fry**." "The current carried the **fry**, head first, downstream, past ducks and herons with hungry beaks, past gulls and dippers eager to feast."

★ "As she swam down the river, her side stripes faded. Her skin secreted a fine mucous coat. Her body grew longer and sleeker and stronger. And one morning she woke to find herself a **smolt**."

★ "She circled the **estuary**, gazed out at the bay, to the water beyond, where her new home lay." "The **estuary** was crowded, she was not alone! Thousands of salmon were headed home."

★ "On sunny days when the sea was filled with a pale green light, Sumi herded herring into sea caves or lazed in beds of **kelp**."

★ "She feasted on sand lance and candlefish and shrimp-like creatures called **krill**!"

Point of View

This is from Sumi the salmon's point of view, from her birth in a small creek, to her time as an adult fish swimming in the sea, and finally, to her return back to where she was born to spawn and die.

Smiley Shark

Ruth Galloway (Tiger Tales, 2005)
ISBN 1-589-25391-4

Smiley Shark was the friendliest of all the fish. He wanted to be friends with and play with the other fish, but all of the other sea creatures were afraid of his big, white teeth. No one wanted to play with him. They all swam away when Smiley Shark came around. When the other sea creatures get trapped in the fisherman's net, Smiley Shark comes to the rescue. He jumps out of the water and smiles at the fisherman. This frightens the fisherman. He drops his net and the sea creatures are freed.

Connecting

Text to World—Some children may have seen a shark or other sea creatures either in an aquarium or in their natural habitats.

Predicting/Anticipating

The fish are trapped. What can Smiley Shark do to help the fish?

Summarizing

This text lends itself well to a retelling.

Story Structure

★ **Characters**—Smiley Shark, puffer fish, starfish, octopus, other fish, fisherman
★ **Setting**—the ocean
★ **Plot**—Smiley Shark wants friends, but all of the sea creatures are afraid of him.
★ **Resolution**—Smiley Shark helps to free the sea creatures from the fisherman's net and they all become friends.

Problem/Solution

★ **Problem**—The fish are trapped.
★ **Solution**—Smiley Shark gets them free by smiling at the fisherman. This scares the fisherman, and he drops his net, freeing the fish.

Sharon Dennis Wyeth (Dragonfly Books, 2002)
ISBN 0-440-41210-2

A young girl growing up in the city yearns to see beyond the dirt, trash, homelessness, and graffiti in her neighborhood. She learns about the word "beautiful" in school, goes on a search for something beautiful, and finds it in many different forms—fried fish sandwiches, a jump rope, beads, new shoes, an apple, a stone, a baby's laugh, and herself. What she comes to understand is that beauty truly lies in the eye of the beholder.

Summarizing/Concluding

★ **Summarizing**—This text lends itself well to a retelling.

★ **Concluding**—What do people see as beautiful in their lives?
Conclusion—The little girl comes to realize that people see beauty in many different ways.

Applying

The reader can look for things that are beautiful in his own life.

Story Structure

★ **Characters**—little girl, teacher, Miss Delphine, girl's friends, Mr. Lee, Mr. Sims, Aunt Carolyn, baby Carl, Mommy

★ **Setting**—her home and neighborhood

★ **Plot**—A little girl tries to find something beautiful in her life. She goes on a search and asks many people what they have that is beautiful.

★ **Resolution**—She finds that each person has something beautiful, but it is not the same for everybody.

Figurative Language

Simile—". . . a broken bottle that looks like fallen stars."

Character Analysis

The author and illustrator give clues to help the reader understand the main character. Facial expressions and body language help the reader understand the character's emotions—sadness, despair, fear, joy, resolve, power, and love.

Theme (Implied)

Although she is growing up in an environment bereft of things commonly thought of as beautiful, the main character is determined to find beauty in her life. What she comes to understand is that beauty looks different to different people. Furthermore, everyone has "something beautiful" in their lives.

Mary Jane and Herm Auch (Holiday House, 2004)
ISBN 0-823-41829-4

Henrietta, a chicken who can read, is so busy reading that she hardly ever lays an egg. Henrietta's aunties aren't laying many eggs, either. The farmer decides to send these old hens on vacation. Henrietta is suspicious when a truck from the Souper Soup Company picks up her aunts for vacation. Because she can read, she knows that her aunts are in trouble. She jumps on the back bumper of the truck but gets blown off. She tries to figure out a way to save them. She goes to a supermarket and finds the address of the Souper Soup Company. She hitches a ride on the back of a truck filled with pigs that were on their way to vacation. Unfortunately, the truck was labeled Saucy Sausage Company. Henrietta warned the pigs and jumped off to continue her search for her aunts. She hitches a ride on another truck filled with cows headed to the Happy Hamburger Company. Again, Henrietta warns the cows and advises them to learn to read because reading can save their lives. Finally, Henrietta meets up with a truck that is also going to the Souper Soup Company. She finds her aunts and frees them. They make a new home with a vegetarian lady who has an organic farm. Henrietta begins a brand new career as a reading teacher.

Summarizing
This text lends itself well to a retelling.

Story Structure
★ **Characters**—Henrietta, her aunts, the farmer, pigs, cows, the vegetarian farmer
★ **Setting**—the farm, the supermarket, the highway, the Souper Soup Company, the organic farm
★ **Plot**—Henrietta's aunts aren't laying many eggs so the farmer is sending them to the soup company where they will be made into soup. She must save them.
★ **Resolution**—Henrietta can read so she finds her aunts, frees them, and begins a new career as a reading teacher.

Problem/Solution

★ **Problem**—Henrietta's aunts are on the truck heading to the soup company. She must figure out where the company is so that she can rescue her aunts.

★ **Solution**—Because Henrietta can read, she is able to locate the factory and free her aunts.

Cause/Effect

Cause—Henrietta can read. **Effect**—She is able to locate her aunts.

Figurative Language

Idiom

- "This is your chance to veg out girls."
- "Yep, just simmer down and relax."

Theme (Implied)

Literacy is a valuable asset. Reading can save your life!

Spiders Are Not Insects

Allan Fowler (Children's Press, 1996)
ISBN 0-516-20219-7

Spiders live almost everywhere. They have been around for a long time; longer than most other animals. Spiders are arachnids, not insects. Spiders come in all sizes. Only a few kinds of spiders are dangerous, although most spiders are poisonous. Many kinds of spiders spin webs, but those that don't spin webs are called hunting spiders. Spiders are helpful to people because they eat harmful insects.

Evaluating/Applying

★ **Evaluating**

- Criterion for comparison—Many people are afraid of spiders.
- Evaluation of text—the author gives objective information about spiders and does not attempt to frighten the reader.

★ **Applying**—Be wary of spiders since most of them are poisonous.

Expository Structure

★ Photographs rather than illustrations
★ Photographs have captions
★ Vocabulary support
★ Index

Main Idea/Details

★ **Main Idea**—Spiders live almost everywhere
  Details
- They live in rain forests.
- They live in deserts.
- They live in water.
- They live in woods.
- They live in gardens.
- They live in people's homes.

★ **Main Idea**—Spiders come in many sizes.
  Details
- Some are so tiny that they can hardly be seen.
- Some are large enough to eat birds and frogs.
- The biggest spiders are tarantulas.

★ ★ ★ ★ CD-104192 ★ Using Children's Literature to Enhance Reading Instruction

★ **Main Idea**—Many spiders use silk to spin webs.
Details
- Different kinds of spiders weave different kinds of webs.
- Webs are sticky.
- Spiders trap insects in webs.

Compare/Contrast
Spiders and insects have similarities and differences.

★ **Similarities**
- They have legs.
- They live in similar places.
- They use specialized body parts to sense the world around them.

★ **Differences**
- Spiders have eight legs; insects have six.
- Spiders do not have wings; insects do.
- Spiders use hairs on their bodies to sense the world; insects use antennae.

Author's Purpose
To inform

Patty Lovell (Putnam Juvenile, 2001)
ISBN 0-399-23416-0

Molly Lou is short and buck-toothed. In addition, she has a terrible singing voice and is often fumble-fingered. In spite of these challenges, her grandmother helps her to believe in herself. All is well until Molly Lou moves to a new school. Teasing from Ronald Durkin starts the first day at the new school and continues unabated. In every situation, Molly Lou remembers what her grandmother has taught her—that she is very capable and is able to overcome. She wins friends in every situation.

Connecting

Text to Self—Some children may have moved to a new school or they know someone who has. Some children may have features that cause others to tease them.

Summarizing

This text lends itself well to a retelling.

Applying

This text can be supportive of students who are new to a school or to those who are anticipating a move.

Story Structure

★ **Characters**—Molly Lou, grandma, Ronald Durkin, school children
★ **Setting**—Grandma's house, new school
★ **Plot**—Molly Lou has some challenges, but her Grandma helps her believe in herself. She moves to a new school and is confronted by Ronald Durkin who is unkind to her.
★ **Resolution**—Molly Lou remembers what her Grandma taught her and is able to stand up to Ronald Durkin.

Figurative Language

★ **Simile**
  • "Molly Lou had a voice that sounded like a bullfrog being squeezed by a boa constrictor."
  • "You sound like a sick duck . . . ."

★ **Hyperbole**—"Molly Lou Melon had buck teeth that stuck out so far, she could stack pennies on them."

★ **Onomatopoeia**—"You sound like a sick duck—Honk Honk!"

Character Analysis

Molly Lou believes in herself despite obvious shortcomings. She is strong, confident, and capable even when the odds are against her.

Janell Cannon (Harcourt Children's Books, 1993)
ISBN 0-152-80217-7

A baby fruit bat is out flying with her mother. They are attacked by an owl that knocks Stellaluna away from her mother and into the air. Stellaluna falls headfirst into a tree where she hangs on until morning. When she can hold on no longer, she falls into a bird's nest. She scoots outside of the nest, but close enough to hear the little birds. After she gets terribly hungry, Stellaluna crawls into the bird's nest. She is raised as a bird even though the birds' diet and ways of living are very foreign to her. After Stellaluna is able to fly on her own, she makes her way back to the area where the bats live and is reunited with her mother.

There is a two-page spread at the back of the book that gives facts about bats.

Connecting

★ **Text to Self**—There may be students who have been separated from their mothers or other caregivers. How did they feel? How did they get reunited with the adults?

★ **Text to Text**—*Zipping, Zapping, Zooming Bats* by Ann Earle (HarperTrophy, 1995)

Summarizing

This text lends itself well to a retelling.

Sequencing

★ Stellaluna and her mother are out flying.
★ They get attacked by an owl.
★ Stellaluna ends up in a bird's nest.
★ Stellaluna is raised as a bird.
★ When she is old enough to fly, Stellaluna flies back to the area where the bats live.
★ Stellaluna finds her mother.

Compare/Contrast

Bats and birds are similar in some ways and different in some ways.

★ **Similarities**
  • Mothers take care of their young.
  • Birds and bats fly.

★ **Differences**
  • Baby birds live in nests; baby bats hang by their feet from trees.
  • Birds eat bugs; bats eat fruit.

- Birds fly during the day; bats fly at night.
- Birds sleep at night; bats sleep during the day.
- Birds land on their feet; bats hang by their feet.

Figurative Language

Simile—"Her baby wings were as limp and useless as wet paper."

Stephanie's Ponytail

Robert Munsch (Annick Press, 1996)
ISBN 1-55037-484-2

Stephanie asks her mother for a ponytail because she wants her hair to be different from the other students in the class. The other kids make fun of her, but the girls wear their hair exactly like Stephanie the next day. She is upset about losing her individuality and tells them that they are all a bunch of copycats. The next day Stephanie has a ponytail in a different place, and the students, again, imitate her hairstyle. Now the girls and some of the boys wear their hair exactly like Stephanie. This pattern continues over several days with Stephanie's ponytail in a different place each day, out of the back, on the side, on the top, out of the front. Each day Stephanie tells the others that they are copycats. After several days of this copycat behavior, Stephanie tells the students that she is going to shave her head. The next day they all come to school and everyone has shaved their heads, except for Stephanie, who has a ponytail coming right out of the back of her head.

This text can be supportive of character education in the area of peer pressure.

Predicting/Anticipating
Readers can predict the other students' reactions and actions when Stephanie comes to school with her ponytail in a different place each day.

Applying
Readers should realize that everyone is an individual and that people should be themselves and not try to copy others.

Story Structure
★ **Characters**—Stephanie, Stephanie's mom, teacher, classmates
★ **Setting**—Stephanie's house, school
★ **Plot**—Stephanie wants her hairstyle to be different. The other students imitate her hairstyle, which greatly upsets Stephanie.
★ **Resolution**—Stephanie tells the class that she is going to shave her head, and that's exactly what the other students do.

Sequencing

★ Stephanie has a ponytail at the back of her head.

★ All of the girls come to school with ponytails at the back.

★ Stephanie has a ponytail on the side of her head.

★ All of the girls and some of the boys come to school with ponytails on the side.

★ Stephanie has a ponytail on the top of her head.

★ All of the girls and all of the boys come to school with ponytails on the top.

★ Stephanie has a ponytail on the front of her head.

★ All of the girls, all of the boys, and the teacher come to school with ponytails on the front.

★ Stephanie tells the class that she is going to shave her head.

★ Everyone comes to school with their heads shaved, except for Stephanie who has a ponytail at the back of her head.

Cause/Effect

★ **Cause**—Stephanie sports a different hairstyle each day. **Effect**—The other students imitate her.

★ **Cause**—Stephanie announces her intent to shave her head. **Effect**—The other students shave their heads.

Figurative Language

Simile—"It looked like broccoli was growing out of their heads."

Character Analysis

Stephanie is a very strong character with actions and language that underscore her traits. She is determined to be unique in her hairstyle. She doesn't want others to imitate her.

Theme (Implied)

Be yourself. Don't imitate others.

The Stray Dog

Marc Simont (HarperTrophy, 2003)
ISBN 0-064-43669-1

A family goes to the park for a picnic. The two children meet a stray dog and play with him, feed him, teach him tricks, and even name him Willy. All week long, each of the family members thinks about Willy. Because they are distracted by thoughts of Willy, each of the family members has mishaps. When they return to the park on the following Saturday, they find Willy again but Willy has a serious problem—the dog warden. The warden is after Willy because he is a stray dog. The children rescue Willy from the dog warden when the girl gives Willy her hair ribbon for a leash and the boy gives Willy his belt for a collar. They take Willy home with them and introduce him to the neighborhood dogs. Willy now has a home.

Connecting

★ **Text to Self**

- Some readers may have seen or adopted a stray dog.
- Some readers may have been to a park for a family picnic.

Predicting/Anticipating

Ask students, "What do you think might happen when the family returns to the park on Saturday?"

Summarizing

This text lends itself well to a retelling.

Story Structure

★ **Characters**—Willy, Mom, Dad, girl, boy, dog warden, neighborhood dogs
★ **Setting**—park, neighborhood where the family lives
★ **Plot**—A stray dog has fun with a family in the park on Saturday. All week, the family thinks of the dog. When they return to the park on Saturday, they encounter Willy again.
★ **Resolution**—Willy comes home to live with the family.

Problem/Solution

★ **Problem**—When the family returns to the park on Saturday, Willy has a problem—the dog warden.
★ **Solution**—The two children solve the problem by telling the warden that Willy belongs to them. They even produce a collar and leash—a hair ribbon and belt.

Cause/Effect

As the family thought about Willy during the week, each of them made mistakes due to their distraction.

★ **Cause**—On Monday, Dad is thinking about Willy. **Effect**—Dad spills his coffee.

★ **Cause**—On Tuesday, the little girl is thinking about Willy. **Effect**—She trips and spills her drink.

★ **Cause**—On Thursday, the little boy is thinking of Willy. **Effect**—He misses the ball.

★ **Cause**—On Friday, Mom is thinking of Willy. **Effect**—She burns dinner.

Picture Clues

Much of the story is embedded in the illustrations—where the family lives, what the children did with Willy at the park, what mistakes are made because they are thinking of Willy, and the bath they give Willy when they take him home.

Colin McNaughton (Voyager Books, 1998)
ISBN 0-152-01699-6

As Preston the pig goes from place to place, Mr. Wolf is hot on his trail. Each time, as Mr. Wolf is preparing to attack, Preston suddenly changes his course of direction causing negative effects for Mr. Wolf. The ending has a wonderful visual surprise.

Predicting/Anticipating

On each page, as Mr. Wolf is preparing to attack Preston, have students predict what Preston might do to avoid being eaten. Turn the page to see if any of their predictions are correct.

Concluding (with Picture Clues)

At the end, Preston tells his mother that he has a feeling that someone has been following him. All you can see of the person he is talking to—who is dressed in his mother's clothing—is a shadow. The shadow looks as though it has two large ears on its head and a hat just like the wolf has been wearing. A conclusion that could be drawn from the picture is that the wolf still hasn't given up. On the next page, the shadow has turned into a full-color picture of Preston's mother with a bandana on her head and she gives Preston a big hug.

Swimmy

Leo Lionni (Dragonfly Books, 1973)
ISBN 0-394-82620-5

Swimmy lives in a happy school of red fish. He is the only black fish in the school. One day, a big tuna swallows the whole school in one gulp. The only survivor is Swimmy. He swims way down deep in the water where he is frightened and lonely. Soon, Swimmy rediscovers the marvels of the ocean and begins a journey during which he encounters all kinds of wonderful sea creatures. He sees a school of little red fish hiding in the rocks and invites them to come swim with him. They are afraid of the big fish, so Swimmy devises a plan. He teaches the little fish how to swim together like one big fish. Swimmy, because he is black, becomes the eye of the big fish. Together, they scare off the big fish.

Predicting/Anticipating
★ What will happen to Swimmy when the tuna eats his school of fish?
★ How will Swimmy help his new friends come out and swim with him?

Summarizing
This text lends itself well to a retelling.

Story structure
★ **Characters**—first school of fish, Swimmy, sea creatures, second school of fish
★ **Setting**—the ocean
★ **Plot**—Swimmy, a single survivor from a school of fish, devises a plan to protect his new friends from the dangers of the big fish that attack smaller fish.
★ **Resolution**—Swimmy teaches them to swim together as one big fish so that the other big fish will be frightened of them.

Problem/Solution
★ **Problem**—Swimmy wants the other little fish to swim and play with him, but they're afraid the big fish will eat them.
★ **Solution**—They all swam together to form a big fish and Swimmy became the eye.

Sequencing
★ Swimmy lives with a happy school of fish.
★ A tuna eats Swimmy's school.
★ Swimmy lives alone in the deep water.

- ★ Swimmy swims about to see the creatures.
- ★ Swimmy meets a new school of fish.
- ★ Swimmy teaches them how to work together to chase away the big fish.

Figurative Language
Simile
- ★ "Only one of them was as black as a mussel shell . . . ."
- ★ " . . . a lobster, who walked about like a water-moving machine . . . ."
- ★ ". . . sea anemones, who looked like pink palm trees . . . ."

Theme (Implied)
When people work together they can solve problems that are insurmountable to an individual working alone.

Margery Cuyler (Henry Holt and Company, 1993)
ISBN 0-805-02954-0

A little boy and his parents go on a trip to the zoo. His parents buy him a shiny red balloon that lifts him up into the air. That's good. No, that's bad. The balloon drifts until it came to a jungle where it breaks on a branch. Thus begins the adventure that takes him through a series of incidents in which he meets many animals and gets into scary situations.

Connecting

Text to Text—*It Could Have Been Worse* by A. H. Benjamin (Little Tiger Press, 2003)

Predicting/Anticipating

When each event occurs and is labeled good or bad, the reader should anticipate why it could be the opposite.

Figurative Language

★ **Simile**—"It was dark as night."

★ **Onomatopoeia**

Some examples are:

- Snake hissed, SSSS
- Giraffe drank, GLUG, GLUG
- Lion snored, ZZZZZ; Lion purred, RRR
- Stork had a drink, SSSSIP

Edith Baer (Scholastic Paperbacks, 1992)
ISBN 0-590-43162-5

From North America to Australia, Edith Baer shares the different ways children get to school—walking; riding the bus, ferry, cable car, horse-and-buggy, trolley, vaporetto, skis, train, bicycle, boat, Metro line, helicopter, or Ski-doo®; roller skating; and jogging. On the last two pages of the book, a map shows the countries where all of the children live.

This book is an excellent tool for beginning instruction in compare/contrast.

Connecting
★ **Text to Self**—Ask students, "How many different ways do you get to school?"
★ **Text to World**—This book brings an awareness of the variety of modes of transportation for school children.

Compare/Contrast
Students can compare and contrast the different ways children in the United States get to school. Then, they can look at the other countries to see if there are any similarities or differences.

Today Was a Terrible Day

Patricia Reilly Giff (Puffin, 1984)
ISBN 0-140-50453-2

Ronald Morgan is having a terrible day; he drops his pencil, eats Jimmy's sandwich, accidentally squirts water on Joy's dress, misses a ball during the game, loses his ice cream money, forgets to water the plants, and knocks the best plant of all off of the window sill. In addition to all of these worries, he is not a very good reader. The day has an uplifting culmination when Ronald Morgan realizes that he can read the note that Miss Tyler sent home with him.

Connecting
★ **Text to Self**—Everyone has had a bad day.
★ **Text to Text**—*Alexander and the Terrible, Horrible, No Good, Very Bad Day* by Judith Viorst (Aladdin Paperbacks, 1978)

Predicting/Anticipating
What is in the note that Miss Tyler sent home?

Summarizing/Concluding
★ **Summarizing**—This text lends itself well to a retelling.
★ **Concluding**
  • What grade is Ronald Morgan in?
    Conclusion—second grade

  • Who is the plant monitor?
    Conclusion—Based on the expression on Ronald Morgan's face and the fact that he has had a terrible day, the reader can conclude that he is the plant monitor.

Story Structure
★ **Characters**—Ronald Morgan, Miss Tyler, Jimmy, Alice, Rosemary, Mrs. Gallop's class, Billy, Michael
★ **Setting**—School, ball field, Ronald Morgan's house
★ **Plot**—Ronald Morgan is having a bad day. Everything goes wrong.
★ **Resolution**—Things turn out okay when he realizes that he can read.

Sequencing
★ Ronald Morgan drops his pencil.
★ Ronald Morgan signs his mother's name.
★ Ronald Morgan eats Jimmy's sandwich.

* Ronald Morgan goes into the hall for a drink of water.
* Ronald Morgan misses the ball.
* Ronald Morgan has trouble reading.
* Ronald Morgan waters the plants and knocks the best one off of the window sill.
* Miss Tyler gives Ronald Morgan a note to take home.
* Ronald Morgan reads the note.

Cause/Effect

* **Cause**—Ronald Morgan crawls under the table looking for his pencil. **Effect**—The children call him Snakey.
* **Cause**—Ronald Morgan spells his mother's name wrong. **Effect**—The children laugh.
* **Cause**—Ronald Morgan eats Jimmy's sandwich. **Effect**—Jimmy cries.
* **Cause**—Ronald Morgan holds his finger over the water faucet. **Effect**—He gets Joy Farley's dress wet.
* **Cause**—Ronald Morgan looks out of the window while watering the plants. **Effect**—He knocks the pot off of the windowsill.
* **Cause**—Ronald Morgan reads the note Miss Tyler sent home. **Effect**—He feels good about himself.

George Shannon (HarperTrophy, 1999)
ISBN 0-688-16424-2

Each letter of the alphabet stands for a word that does not begin with that specific letter, but represents something that the word will become. "A is for seed—tomorrow's apple. B is for eggs—tomorrow's birds."

This text requires the reader to look beyond the obvious and to think about the possibilities.

Connecting

★ **Text to Text**

- *Q is for Duck: An Alphabet Guessing Game* by Mary Elting and Michael Folsom (Houghton Mifflin Company, 2005)
- Traditional alphabet books

Predicting/Anticipating

What will each of the items become that begins with the appropriate letter?

Applying

Let students make their own alphabet books.

Too Many Pumpkins

Linda White (Holiday House, 1997)
ISBN 0-823-41320-9

Rebecca Estelle hates pumpkins. Her family experienced some hard times when she was younger, and all they had to eat was pumpkins. She decided she would never eat or even look at pumpkins again. Then, a pumpkin delivery truck accidentally drops a pumpkin in her front yard. She tries to dig it up and cover it up, but it continues to grow and grow in spite of her. Rebecca Estelle decides to use only the back door and not even look at the pumpkin vine. It grows and grows until the whole front yard is covered with pumpkins. To get rid of all of those pumpkins, Rebecca makes all kinds of pumpkin treats and gives them away to the townspeople. All she keeps is a handful of pumpkin seeds to plant in the spring.

Connecting

Text to Self—Most people have some food that they particularly dislike.

Predicting/Anticipating

Ask students, "What is happening to the pumpkin vine while Rebecca Estelle is ignoring it?"

Summarizing

This text lends itself well to a retelling.

Problem/Solution

★ **Problem**—Rebecca Estelle has pumpkins growing all over the front yard.
★ **Solution**—She makes pumpkin treats for the townspeople.

Sequencing

★ Rebecca Estelle grows vegetables, but not pumpkins.
★ A truck drops a pumpkin in her front yard.
★ Rebecca Estelle ignores the pumpkin.
★ Pumpkins grow all over the front yard.
★ Rebecca Estelle makes treats out of the pumpkins.
★ Rebecca Estelle makes a jack-o'-lantern out of a pumpkin.
★ The townspeople come.
★ Rebecca Estelle keeps a handful of seeds for planting in the spring.

Figurative Language

★ **Metaphor**
  • "The entire yard was a sea of plump, round pumpkins."
  • "The seeds were a mountain in the corner."

A Tree Is Nice

Janice May Udry (HarperTrophy, 1987)
ISBN 0-064-43147-9

If you are a tree lover, you will especially enjoy this book. It begins with a very simple sentence and then elaborates on the importance of a tree, listing many of the wonderful things it has to offer.

Main Idea/Details

This is an excellent book to teach beginning main idea/details.

★ **Main Idea**—Trees are very nice.
Details
- Trees make woods.
- Trees have leaves.
- Trees have trunks and limbs.
- You can play in trees.
- Birds build nests in trees.
- Trees provide shade.

Theme (Implied)

The importance of trees

Unlovable

Dan Yaccarino (Henry Holt and Company, 2002)
ISBN 0-805-06321-8

Alfred feels that no one loves him. All of the household and neighborhood animals confirm his belief by telling him the many ways in which they find him inadequate. One day, a family moves in next door, and they have a dog. Alfred tells Rex, the new dog, that he is a golden retriever. As Alfred and Rex get to know each other from opposite sides of the fence, they become friends. One day, Rex digs under the fence and the two dogs see each other face to face for the first time. They look exactly alike. They play together, and Alfred never feels unlovable again.

Summarizing
This text lends itself well to a retelling.

Inferring
Why did Alfred say that he was a golden retriever?

Story Structure
★ **Characters**—Alfred, cat, parrot, goldfish, German shepherd, greyhound, poodle, Doberman, Rex
★ **Setting**—Alfred's house and yard, Rex's yard
★ **Plot**—Alfred feels unloved and spends much of his time alone. A new dog moves in next door. They become friends across the fence. Eventually, Alfred finds out that he and the new dog look just alike.
★ **Resolution**—Alfred never feels unlovable again.

Problem/Solution
★ **Problem**—Alfred feels unlovable.
★ **Solution**—Rex moves in next door and they become friends.

Cause/Effect
Cause—Rex is digging under the fence so that he and Alfred can meet. **Effect**—Alfred hides.

Point of View
Alfred feels very inadequate because of all the other animals' teasing.

★ ★ ★ ★ CD-104192 ★ **Using Children's Literature to Enhance Reading Instruction**

Margery Williams (Grosset & Dunlap, 1987)
ISBN 0-448-19083-4

A boy gets a velveteen rabbit one Christmas. He plays with him for about two hours and then forgets about him. The other nursery animals try to help the rabbit understand what it means to be real. One night, because he can't find his favorite china dog, the boy sleeps with the rabbit. From then on, the rabbit sleeps with the boy. Because he loves him so much, the rabbit becomes real for the boy. After the boy has a bout with scarlet fever, all of the toys and books that he has played with must be destroyed. The rabbit cries a real tear, and where the tear falls, a flower grows. The nursery fairy steps out of the flower and turns the stuffed rabbit into a real rabbit. Now, he can jump and play just as the other rabbits in the garden do. One day when the boy goes to play in the woods, he sees a real rabbit that reminds him very much of his beloved stuffed rabbit.

Connecting
★ **Text to Self**—Many children have stuffed animals that are very special to them.
★ **Text to Text**—*Betty Doll* by Patricia Polacco (Philomel Books, 2001)

Summarizing
This text lends itself well to a retelling.

Inferring
Why couldn't the boy sleep without the velveteen rabbit?

Story Structure
★ **Characters**—the boy, the velveteen rabbit, other nursery toys, Nana, garden rabbits, the doctor, nursery magic fairy
★ **Setting**—the boy's home, the garden
★ **Plot**—A boy loves a velveteen rabbit so much that it becomes real for him. After a bout with scarlet fever, the rabbit must be destroyed. The nursery fairy turns the velveteen rabbit into a real rabbit.
★ **Resolution**—The boy sees a rabbit in the garden, but doesn't realize that it is his old friend.

Problem/Solution
★ **Problem**—The toy rabbit must be burned because he was with the boy when he had scarlet fever.
★ **Solution**—The nursery fairy takes him away to become a real rabbit.

Cause/Effect
Cause—The toy rabbit is with the boy when he has scarlet fever. **Effect**—The toy rabbit must be burned.

The Wednesday Surprise

Eve Bunting (Clarion Books, 1989)
ISBN 0-395-54776-8

Every Wednesday night, Grandma comes to Anna's house. She brings a big, heavy bag with her. They sit on the couch and read books together. They are preparing a special surprise for Dad's birthday on Saturday. Dad, who is a truck driver, comes home on Saturday. They have the special birthday celebration, and then, Grandma and Anna give their special present. Grandma takes one of the books and begins to read. The special present is that Anna has taught Grandma to read.

Connecting
Text to Self—Some students may know adults who cannot read or who are learning to read.

Predicting/Anticipating
As Anna and Grandma make preparations for Dad's birthday, the reader should be trying to figure out what the big surprise is.

Summarizing/Concluding
★ **Summarizing**—This text lends itself well to a retelling.

★ **Concluding**
   • What is in the big, cloth bag that Grandma is carrying?
     Conclusion—The bag is filled with books.

Inferring
★ Why does Dad come home on Saturday night?
★ Why are Mom, Dad, and Sam astonished when Grandma starts reading?
★ Why are Dad's eyes brimming over with tears?

Story Structure
★ **Characters**—Grandma, Anna, Sam, Mom, Dad
★ **Setting**—Anna's apartment
★ **Plot**—Grandma and Anna are planning a special surprise for Dad's birthday. Grandma is learning to read after years of being encouraged to do so by her son. Anna is teaching her.
★ **Resolution**—Grandma's special present for Dad is that she reads for him on his birthday.

Figurative Language
★ **Simile**—"Only seven years old and smart as paint already."
★ **Hyperbole**
   • "'What have you got in this bag, Grandma? Bricks?'"
   • "'Maybe I will read everything in the world now that I've started.'"

★ ★ ★ ★   CD-104192 ★ **Using Children's Literature to Enhance Reading Instruction**

Wemberly Worried

Kevin Henkes (Greenwillow, 2000)
ISBN 0-688-17027-7

A mouse named Wemberly worries about everything—little things and big things. Most of all she worries about her doll, Petal. As she anticipates the first day of school, she realizes that she has a whole list of new things to worry about. Wemberly meets a new friend who is much like herself. Wemberly and Jewel gradually get to know each other and, eventually, become friends. Wemberly worries less.

This book is a valuable resource for helping to relieve anxieties, particularly at the beginning of school.

Connecting

★ **Text to Self**—Most students will relate to times when they have been worried about something.
★ **Text to Text**
   • *Worry Wart Wes* by Tolya L. Thompson (Savor Publishing House, 2002)
   • *Stop Drop and Roll* by Margery Cuyler (Simon & Schuster Children's, 2001)

Predicting/Anticipating

What might Wemberly worry about concerning school?

Summarizing

This text lends itself well to a retelling.

Story Structure

★ **Characters**—Wemberly, Mom, Dad, grandmother, Petal, Jewel, Mrs. Peachum, Nibblet
★ **Setting**—Wemberly's house, school
★ **Plot**—Wemberly worries all the time. Her family is concerned about her. She worries about starting school. Wemberly meets a friend and is happy at school.
★ **Resolution**—She doesn't worry as much.

Cause/Effect

Cause—Wemberly meets Jewel. **Effect**—Wemberly worries less.

Character Analysis

★ What is Wemberly like at the beginning of the story?

★ How does Wemberly change after she gets to know Jewel?

★ What is Wemberly like at the end of the story?

Picture Clues

Some of the illustrations have captions that explain the things that cause Wemberly to worry.

★ **Big Things**—illustration shows her mother and father

   Caption—"I wanted to make sure you were still here."

Theme (Implied)

Try not to worry. Just be happy.

Carolyn Otto (HarperTrophy, 1996)
ISBN 0-064-45160-7

Everywhere, all the time, animals are hunting or being hunted. Colors and camouflage help an animal survive. The concept of animal disguise is explored through engaging text and detailed illustrations. Many animals, both prey and predators, are examined. Animal camouflage is a disguise that makes an animal hard to see. It helps animals hide from enemies or helps a predator sneak up on prey. Both hunting and hiding are easier when an animal matches its surroundings. Some animals disguise themselves by decorating their bodies, others by changing colors. Colors can also serve to attract attention or warn predators. Harmless animals copy the color patterns of other harmful animals in an attempt to frighten off enemies.

This book fits well with a science unit about animals.

Applying
The reader can look for camouflaging in the animals in their environment.

Expository Structure
Illustrations with labels

Cause/Effect
★ **Cause**—An animal's coloration helps it blend in with its surroundings. **Effect**—It is easier for animals to hunt and hide.

★ **Cause**—Animals use bright colors or patterns to warn predators. **Effect**—Predators avoid these animals.

★ **Cause**—Harmless animals mimic the colors of harmful animals. **Effect**—Predators avoid these animals.

Main Idea/Details
★ **Main Idea**—Camouflage makes animals hard to see.
Details—This text includes many details about animal coloration. Here are a few examples:
* A mountain lion's fur matches the grass.
* A fawn's spots match the sun and shade that dapple the thicket.
* A ptarmigan changes the colors of her feathers with the seasons.

Author's Purpose
To inform

What! Cried Granny: An Almost Bedtime Story

Kate Lum (Puffin Books, 2002)
ISBN 0-142-30092-6

Patrick is going to stay all night with Granny for the first time. The problem begins at bedtime when Granny tells him it is time to get ready for bed and Patrick informs her that he doesn't have a bed. Granny frantically runs to the front yard, cuts down a tree, and makes Patrick a bed. When she tells Patrick that he now can go to bed, he informs her that he doesn't have a pillow. Granny quickly runs out to the henhouse, collects feathers, sews a bag, stuffs it with feathers, and gives Patrick a new pillow. However, Patrick still can't go to bed as his problems continue—he doesn't have a cover  (Granny makes it from sheep wool) or a Teddy Bear (Granny makes it from her curtains). Finally, when a tired Granny, who has lost her patience, has made Patrick everything he needs and orders him to go to bed, he informs her that it is morning.

The illustrations add to the text and show each step that Granny takes in making the item for Patrick. Students are shown how down pillows are made and how blankets are woven from sheep's wool.

Sequencing

This book allows for several different sequencing opportunities. Students can list the items Granny has to make to meet Patrick's bedtime needs and sequence the order in which she makes them. Students can also use the text and picture clues to sequence the steps Granny takes to make each of the items.

★ Sequencing the items in the order they were made:
- Granny makes a bed.
- Granny makes a pillow.
- Granny makes a blanket.
- Granny makes a teddy bear.

Here are two examples of sequencing the steps Granny takes to make the items:

★ Granny made a bed.
- Granny chops down a tree.
- Granny cuts the log into lumber.
- Granny measures the wood.
- Granny drills the wood.
- Granny nails the wood.
- Granny paints the bed.
- Granny put a mattress on the bed.

★ Granny made a blanket.
- Granny shears the sheep.
- Granny spins the wool into yarn.
- She knits the blanket.
- She dyes the blanket purple.

Author's Purpose

★ To entertain
★ To explain how particular items are made

May Garelick (Mondo Publishing, 1995)
ISBN 1-572-55008-2

The characteristics that birds share with other animals are pointed out. Birds build nests, fly, and lay eggs, but so do other kinds of animals. The one characteristic that birds have that no other living creature has is feathers.

Main Idea/Details

★ **Main Idea**—Even though birds share characteristics with other animals, only birds have feathers.

Details

- Many animals fly, like birds.
- Some birds can't fly.
- Some insects have wings, but they aren't birds.
- Other creatures sing, but they aren't birds.
- Not all birds build nests.
- Other animals, besides birds, lay eggs.

Author's Purpose

To inform

Context Clues

molt, **camouflaged**

★ "About once a year, birds **molt**."

★ "But the eggs are the color of the sand around them—**camouflaged**—so they are safe."

★ ★ ★ ★ CD-104192 ★ Using Children's Literature to Enhance Reading Instruction

Lynda DeWitt (HarperTrophy, 1993)
ISBN 0-064-45113-5

How do meteorologists make weather forecasts? What are the factors that determine the weather at any given place on Earth? This text gives information about cold and warm fronts, air temperature, air movement, humidity, and air pressure. All of these factors contribute to the weather conditions.

Evaluating/Applying

★ **Evaluating**
  - **Criterion for Comparison**—Many complex factors contribute to current weather conditions.
  - **Evaluation of Text**—Readers are presented with information about how weather forecasts are formulated in an easy-to-understand format with illustrations that are very supportive.

★ **Applying**—Readers should watch weather forecasts so that they will be able to plan what to wear, when to have outdoor activities, etc.

Expository Structure

★ Illustration with labels
★ Text accompanied by captions
★ Map

Cause/Effect

★ **Cause**—Air rises into the sky when air pressure is low. **Effect**—Rain or snow may fall.
★ **Cause**—Air pressure is high most of the time. **Effect**—Skies stay mostly clear.
★ **Cause**—Meteorologists make forecasts. **Effect**—People can plan their activities.

Main Idea/Details

★ **Main Idea**—Meteorologists study many factors in order to determine what the weather will be.
  Details
  - Most changes in the weather occur along fronts.
  - Meteorologists predict where fronts will form.
  - Meteorologists measure the humidity in the air.
  - Meteorologists measure air pressure.
  - Meteorologists study maps to forecast the weather.
  - Forecasts tell us what kind of weather is coming.

Author's Purpose

To inform

Molly Bang (Scholastic Paperbacks, 2004)
ISBN 0-439-59845-1

Sophie gets angry sometimes. When her sister grabs her toy away from her, Sophie has to learn to deal with her anger. She kicks, she screams, she runs, and she cries. Now that she has vented, she begins to become aware of the world around her. Familiar things in her world comfort her. She feels better and heads for home.

This text can be a helpful resource to use when teaching character development.

Connecting
★ **Text to Self**—Everyone has been angry at some time.
★ **Text to World**—Many people have special places they go to when they need to be comforted.

Evaluating/Applying
★ **Evaluating**
  • **Criterion for Comparison**—Some people have a difficult time dealing with anger.
  • **Evaluation of Text**—The author gives readers a practical way to cope with anger.

★ **Applying**—What are some things you can do to dispel your anger?

Figurative Language
Hyperbole—"She roars a red, red roar."

Theme (Implied)
People handle anger in different ways.

Widget

Lyn Rossiter McFarland (Farrar, Straus and Giroux, 2006)
ISBN 0-374-48386-8

Widget is a stray dog that has no home or friends. He sees Mrs. Diggs' home where she has six cats—all girls. Widget desperately wants to become a part of this family. Widget imitates the behavior of the cats in order to trick them and be accepted. He is successful and fits right in with Mrs. Diggs and the girls. One day, Mrs. Diggs has an accident and Widget needs to bark in order to draw attention and get help. When Widget barks, everyone comes and Mrs. Diggs is saved.

This text makes a humorous connection to the scientific concept of adaptation.

Summarizing/Concluding

★ **Summarizing**—This text lends itself well to a retelling.

★ **Concluding**
  • Who are the girls?
    Conclusion—The cats are the girls.

Inferring—Why do the cats puff up, hiss, spit, and growl?

Story Structure

★ **Characters**—Widget, the cats, Mrs. Diggs, people who came to help Mrs. Diggs
★ **Setting**—Mrs. Diggs's house
★ **Plot**—A homeless dog makes changes in his behavior so that he can fit in with a family of cats. When Mrs. Diggs has a problem, he has to resort to barking in order to summon help.
★ **Resolution**—Help comes and Mrs. Diggs is saved.

Problem/Solution

★ **Problem**—Widget is homeless, cold, and hungry.
★ **Solution**—He solves his problem by imitating the cats so he can become part of the family.

★ **Problem**—Mrs. Diggs is hurt and needs help.
★ **Solution**—Widget barks and help comes.

Compare/Contrast

Dogs and cats are alike in some ways and different in other ways.

★ **Similarities**

- Dogs and cats want homes.
- Dogs and cats need food.
- Dogs and cats make sounds.

★ **Differences**

- Dogs bark; cats meow.
- Dogs growl; cats purr.
- Cats use a litter box; dogs don't.
- Cats climb trees; dogs don't.

Context Clues

screeched, **yowled**, **caterwauled**

"They **screeched**. They **yowled**. They **caterwauled** for help."

Picture Clues

Refer to the page where Widget is in the tree with the cats. The text says that sometimes Widget forgets that he is a dog.

James Marshall (Houghton Mifflin Company, 2003)
ISBN 0-618-31659-0

Harriet and Winnie are very different. Harriet reads, has many hobbies, and stays busy all day. On the other hand, Winnie is bored. When offered a ride in a hot air balloon, Winnie accepts, never noticing that the pilot is a fox. And so the adventure begins. Winnie has many very narrow escapes, as, all the while, Harriet is busy trying to rescue her from the fox.

Summarizing

This text lends itself well to a retelling.

Inferring

★ Why did Mr. Johnson say that plump is nice?
★ Why would the grey fox try to help Winnie escape from Mr. Johnson?
★ Why did Harriet put Winnie to bed with a book?

Character Analysis

Harriet is sensible and likes to stay busy with reading and hobbies. Winnie is bored and looks for wild adventures that are dangerous.

Theme (Implied)

Reading introduces readers to the world with its many wonders and dangers.

Wolf

Becky Bloom (Scholastic, Inc., 1999)
ISBN 0-531-30155-9

A hungry wolf pays a visit to a farm with hopes of finding his next meal. The animals at the farm ignore the howling wolf telling him to go somewhere else because they are educated animals and are trying to read. Wolf thinks that maybe he could learn to read, too. He goes to school, visits the library, and goes to the bookstore to buy his very own book. So begins his journey into the next stage of his life when he becomes a literate wolf.

Summarizing
This text lends itself well to a retelling.

Inferring
Why is the wolf's behavior different each time he goes back to the farm?

Story Structure
★ **Characters**—wolf, pig, duck, cow
★ **Setting**—the farm, the school, the library, a bookshop
★ **Plot**—A hungry wolf goes to the farm to find food, but finds literate animals instead. He begins his quest to learn to read.
★ **Resolution**—When he finally can read, he goes back to the farm and reads story after story to the other animals.

Sequencing
★ Wolf goes to the farm looking for food.
★ The animals shoo him away, telling him that they are trying to read.
★ The wolf goes to school to try to learn to read.
★ The wolf goes to the library to learn to read.
★ The wolf buys his very own book.
★ The wolf goes back to the farm and reads story after story to the other animals.

Character Analysis
Wolf undergoes several changes of attitude during the course of this tale. Readers should be alert to word choice and illustrations that indicate his metamorphosis. At the beginning, he is dangerous and leaps at the farm animals with a howl. As he progresses in his literacy, he visits the farm and jumps over the fence, then, he knocks at the farm gate. Finally, he rings the bell.

Theme (Implied)
Literacy changes lives.

★ ★ ★ ★   CD-104192 ★ **Using Children's Literature to Enhance Reading Instruction**

Brenda Parkes (Rigby, 2000)
ISBN 0-763-52962-1

This rhyming book tells the story of the three little pigs from the wolf's perspective. The wolf tells us that the story the pigs told just wasn't true. When he blew down the pigs' houses, he was trying to be helpful. He only wanted to show them that their houses were not strong enough. Fairy tale characters appear to help point out the salient facts.

Connecting

Text to Text—*The Three Little Pigs* by Steven Kellogg (HarperCollins Publishers, 2002)

Summarizing

This text lends itself well to a retelling.

Point of View

The wolf tells how he was just trying to be helpful.

Editor's Note: This title is available through the Rigby Web site: *http://rigby.harcourtachieve.com.*

Joan Rankin (Aladdin, 2001)
ISBN 0-689-84047-0

Lillee was the last duck to hatch. She was also the smallest and skinniest of all. Her brothers and sisters were already swimming, but Lillee was too afraid. She was only interested in learning to walk. Her mother warned her about the fox, but Lillee didn't heed her advice. While walking in the forest, Lillee met Mr. Furry-legs. She eventually discovers that Mr. Furry-legs is the fox that is trying to fatten her up before he eats her. Lillee has to get away, so she runs, then swims, and, finally, flies out of reach.

Predicting/Anticipating
Ask students, "Who is Mr. Furry-legs?"

Summarizing
This text lends itself well to a retelling.

Story Structure
★ **Characters**—Lillee, Lillee's mother, Lillee's brothers and sisters, Mr. Fox

★ **Setting**—pond, forest, bigger pond

★ **Plot**—Lillee is afraid to swim and fly, but her encounter with Mr. Fox forces her to swim and then fly in order to escape.

★ **Resolution**—Lillee finds that she can swim and fly just like the other ducks.

Problem/Solution
★ **Problem**—Lillee realizes that the "friend" who has been trying to fatten her up is really Mr. Fox.

★ **Solution**—Lillee finds out that she can do what other ducks do—swim and fly.

Sequencing
★ Lillee hatches from her egg.

★ Lillee did not want her feet off the ground.

★ Lillee practiced walking.

★ She met Mr. Furry-legs on one of her walks.

★ Mr. Furry-legs shows her where the nasturtium leaves were.

★ Lillee meets Mr. Furry-legs-Long-tail.

★ Mr. Furry-legs-Long-tail shows Lillee where the wild berries are.

★ Lillee meets Mr. Furry-legs-Long-tail-Sharp-snout.

★ Mr. Furry-legs-Long-tail-Sharp-snout shows Lillee where to find snails.

★ Lillee meets Mr. Furry-legs-Long-tail-Sharp-snout-Pink-tongue.

- ★ Mr. Furry-legs-Long-tail-Sharp-snout-Pink-tongue tries to lure Lillee further into the forest.
- ★ Lillee realizes that this is Mr. Fox.
- ★ Lillee runs, swims, and flies to escape from Mr. Fox.

Context Clues

admire, **coaxed**, **stroll**, **scrumptious**

- ★ "She wanted *everyone* to **admire** tiny Lillee."
- ★ "'Come along, Lillee,' **coaxed** Mother Duck."
- ★ "'Let's **stroll** together into the forest.'"
- ★ "The snails were so tasty, so absolutely **scrumptious** . . ."

Picture Clues

Each time Mr. Fox's name grows, more of him is revealed in the illustrations.

Ann Earle (HarperTrophy, 1995)
ISBN 0-064-45133-X

Did you know that the brown bat can catch 150 mosquitoes in 15 minutes and the gray bat can eat 3,000 insects in one night? This book is filled with bat facts that will surprise readers and make them want to learn more about this strange mammal. At the end of the book, students will find two pages filled with bat facts. The last page has instructions for building a bat house.

Connecting

★ **Text to Self**—Ask students, "Have you ever seen a bat?"

★ **Text to Text**—*Stellaluna* by Janell Cannon (Scholastic, Inc., 1993)

★ **Text to World**—Discuss with the class what they might do to help protect bats. Also, what type of bats might you find in your area?

Expository Structure

★ Additional bat information on pages 30 and 31
★ Instructions for building a bat house on page 32

Main Idea/Details

This book is focused around a variety of supporting details concerning bats. Here are a few examples:

★ **Main idea**—Bats are terrific hunters.
   Details
   • "A little brown bat can catch 150 mosquitoes in 15 minutes."
   • "The gray bat can gobble 3,000 insects in one night."
   • The 20,000,000 Mexican free-tailed bats in Bracken Cave in Texas munch 250 tons of insects every night.
   • Bats use echolocation to help them quickly find their prey.
   • Bats are expert fliers.

★ **Main idea**—"In winter, many bats hibernate."
Details
- "The bats are deeply sleeping.
- ". . . their breathing slows down."
- ". . . their heart rate drops from 900 to 20 beats a minute."
- Hibernating bats need less energy to stay alive.
- Bats get ready to hibernate by eating a lot of food and their bodies store the extra food as fat.

★ **Main idea**—Bats are being harmed.
Details
- Their caves are being disturbed.
- People are destroying their homes.
- "People close off their attics and tear down old barns."
- "People seal off empty mines and cut down forests."

★ **Main idea**—People can help save bats.
Details
- They can put bat houses in their yards.
- Public parks and nature centers can put up bat houses.
- Some groups are putting gates on caves so bats can fly through the gates, but people can't get through.

Author's Purpose
To inform readers of facts about bats and how people can help protect them

References

Children's Books Cited

101 Facts about Iguanas by Sarah Williams (Gareth Stevens Publishing, 2001)

A. Lincoln and Me by Louise Borden (Scholastic Paperbacks, 2001)

Agatha's Feather Bed by Carmen Agra Deedy (Peachtree Publishers, 1994)

Alexander and the Terrible, Horrible, No Good, Very Bad Day by Judith Viorst (Aladdin Paperbacks, 1972)

Alexander, Who Used to be Rich Last Sunday by Judith Viorst (Aladdin, 1987)

Amazing Grace by Mary Hoffman (Dial Books, 1991)

Annie and the Old One by Miska Miles (Little, Brown and Company, 1985)

Annie and the Wild Animals by Jan Brett (Houghton Mifflin Company, 1989)

Arnie the Doughnut by Laurie Keller (Henry Holt and Company, 2003)

A Bad Case of Stripes by David Shannon (Scholastic Paperbacks, 2004)

Baloney (Henry P.) by Jon Scieszka and Lane Smith (Puffin, 2005)

Because a Little Bug Went Ka-Choo! by Rosetta Stone (Random House Books for Young Readers, 1975)

Because Brian Hugged His Mother by David L. Rice (Dawn Publications, 1999)

Bedhead by Margie Palatini (Aladdin, 2003)

Betty Doll by Patricia Polacco (Philomel Books, 2001)

Biggest, Strongest, Fastest by Steve Jenkins (Houghton Mifflin Company, 1997)

Book! Book! Book! by Deborah Bruss (Arthur A. Levine Books, 2001)

Boundless Grace by Mary Hoffman (Puffin, 2000)

Brown Bear, Brown Bear, What Do You See? by Bill Martin Jr. (Holt, Rinehart, and Winston, 1967)

Bubble Gum, Bubble Gum by Lisa Wheeler (Little, Brown and Company, 2004)

Chester the Out-of-Work-Dog by Marilyn Singer (Henry Holt and Company, 1997)

Chickens Aren't The Only Ones by Ruth Heller (Putnam Juvenile, 1999)

Cinderella by Charles Perrault (Seastar Books, 2000)

Click, Clack, Moo: Cows That Type by Doreen Cronin (Simon and Schuster, 2000)

Dandelions by Eve Bunting (Voyager Books, 2001)

Don't Need Friends by Carolyn Crimi (Dragonfly Books, 2001)

Dory Story by Jerry Pallotta (Charlesbridge Publishing, 2004)

The Easter Egg Farm by Mary Jane Auch (Holiday House, 1994)

Felix Travels Back in Time by Annette Langen (Parklane Publishing, 2004)

Finklehopper Frog by Irene Livingston (Tricycle Press, 2003)

First Day Jitters by Julie Danneberg (Charlesbridge Publishing, 2000)

The Frog Prince adapted by Jon Scieszka from the Brothers Grimm (Penguin Putnam Books for Young Readers, 1994)

Gasp! The Breathtaking Adventures of a Fish Left Home Alone by Terry Denton (Penguin Global, 2004)

The Giant Hug by Sandra Horning (Knopf Books for Young Readers, 2005)

Giggle, Giggle, Quack by Doreen Cronin (Simon & Schuster Children's Publishing, 2002)

Giraffes Can't Dance by Giles Andreae (Orchard Books, 2001)

Give Maggie a Chance by Frieda Wishinsky (Fitzhenry & Whiteside Limited, 2002)

Grandpa's Teeth by Rod Clement (HarperTrophy, 1999)

Green Wilma by Tedd Arnold (Puffin, 1998)

Hey, Mama Goose by Jane Breskin Zalben (Dutton Juvenile, 2005)

The Honest-to-Goodness Truth by Patricia C. McKissack (Aladdin, 2003)

Hooway for Wodney Wat by Helen Lester (Houghton Mifflin Company, 2002)

Hottest, Coldest, Highest, Deepest by Steve Jenkins (Houghton Mifflin Company, 2004)

A House for Hermit Crab by Eric Carle (Aladdin, 2002)

How Is a Moose Like a Goose? by Robin Michal Koontz (Millbrook Press, 2002)

How Will We Get to the Beach? by Brigitte Luciani (North-South Books, 2000)

I Ain't Gonna Paint No More by Karen Beaumont (Harcourt Children's Books, 2005)

I Wanna Iguana by Karen Kaufman Orloff (G. P. Putnam's Sons, 2004)

I Went Walking by Sue Williams (Voyager Books, 1992)

If You Give a Mouse a Cookie by Laura Numeroff (HarperCollins Children's Books, 1985)

Ira Sleeps Over by Bernard Waber (Houghton Mifflin Company, 1975)

Is It Larger? Is It Smaller? by Tana Hoban (HarperTrophy, 1997)

It Could Have Been Worse by A. H. Benjamin (Little Tiger Press, 2003)

It Wasn't My Fault by Helen Lester (Houghton Mifflin Company, 1989)

Just Like You and Me by David Miller (Dial Books for Young Readers, 2001)

Just One More Story by Dugald Steer (Dutton Children's Books, 1999)

Liar, Liar, Pants on Fire by Diane deGroat (SeaStar Books, 2003)

The Listening Walk by Paul Showers (HarperTrophy, 1993)

Little Red Riding Hood by The Brothers Grimm (Penguin Putnam Books for Young Readers, 1991)

The Little Scarecrow Boy by Margaret Wise Brown (HarperTrophy, 2005)

A Log's Life by Wendy Pfeffer (Simon & Schuster Children's Publishing, 1997)

Loki and Alex: The Adventures of a Dog and His Best Friend by Charles R. Smith, Jr. (Dutton Juvenile, 2001)

Mama, If You Had a Wish by Jeanne Modesitt (Aladdin, 1999)

Mike and the Bike by Michael Ward (Cookie Jar Publishing, 2005)

Missing: One Stuffed Rabbit by Maryann Cocca-Leffler (Albert Whitman & Company, 2000)

The Monster at the End of This Book by Jon Stone (Random House Children's Books, 2004)

More Parts by Tedd Arnold (Puffin, 2003)

More True Lies: 18 Tales for You to Judge by George Shannon (Greenwillow, 2001)

My Great-Aunt Arizona by Gloria Houston (HarperTrophy, 1997)

My Teacher Sleeps in School by Leatie Weiss (Puffin, 1985)

Never, Ever Shout in a Zoo by Karma Wilson (Little, Brown and Company, 2004)

Night Noises by Mem Fox (Voyager Books, 1992)

Night Tree by Eve Bunting (Voyager Books, 1994)

Once There Was a Bull . . . (frog) by Rick Walton (Putnam Juvenile, 1998)

One Smile by Cindy McKinley (Illumination Arts Publishing, Inc., 2002)

Oops! A Preston Pig Story by Colin McNaughton (Voyager Books, 2000)

Ordinary Mary's Extraordinary Deed by Emily Pearson (Gibbs Smith, 2002)

Our Granny by Margaret Wild (Houghton Mifflin Company, 1998)

The Pain and the Great One by Judy Blume (Dragonfly Books, 1985)

The Paperboy by Dav Pilkey (Orchard Books, 1999)

Peter Pan by J. M. Barrie (Dover Publications, 1999)

A Present for Mom by Vivian French (Candlewick, 2005)

The Prince and the Pauper by Mark Twain (Tor Books, 1992)

Q is for Duck by Mary Elting and Michael Folsom (Houghton Mifflin Company, 2005)

A Quiet Place by Douglas Wood (Aladdin, 2005)

Salmon Creek by Annette LeBox and Karen Reczuch (Groundwood Books, 2005)

Simon Can't Say Hippopotamus by Bonnie Highsmith Taylor (Mondo Publishing, 2003)

Smiley Shark by Ruth Galloway (Tiger Tales, 2005)

Something Beautiful by Sharon Dennis Wyeth (Dragonfly Books, 2002)

Souperchicken by Mary Jane and Herm Auch (Holiday House, 2004)

Spiders Are Not Insects by Allan Fowler (Children's Press, 1996)

Stand Tall, Molly Lou Melon by Patty Lovell (Putnam Juvenile, 2001)

Stellaluna by Janell Cannon (Harcourt Children's Books, 1993)

Stephanie's Ponytail by Robert Munsch (Annick Press, 1996)

Stop Drop and Roll by Margery Cuyler (Simon & Schuster Children's, 2001)

The Stray Dog by Marc Simont (HarperTrophy, 2003)

Suddenly! A Preston Pig Story by Colin McNaughton (Voyager Books, 1998)

Swimmy by Leo Lionni (Dragonfly Books, 1973)

That's Good! That's Bad! by Margery Cuyler (Henry Holt and Company, 1993)

This Is the Way We Go to School: A Book about Children around the World by Edith Baer (Scholastic Paperbacks, 1992)

The Three Little Pigs by Steven Kellogg (HarperCollins Publishers, 2002)

Time for a Tale by Dugald Steer (Penguin Putnam Books for Young Readers, 2002)

Today Was a Terrible Day by Patricia Reilly Giff (Puffin, 1984)

Tomorrow's Alphabet by George Shannon (HarperTrophy, 1999)

Too Many Pumpkins by Linda White (Holiday House, 1997)

A Tree Is Nice by Janice May Udry (HarperTrophy, 1987)

The Ugly Duckling by Hans Christian Anderson (William Morrow & Company, 1999)

Unlovable by Dan Yaccarino (Henry Holt and Company, 2002)

The Velveteen Rabbit by Margery Williams (Grosset & Dunlap, 1987)

The Wednesday Surprise by Eve Bunting (Clarion Books, 1989)

Wemberly Worried by Kevin Henkes (Greenwillow, 2000)

What Color Is Camouflage? by Carolyn Otto (HarperTrophy, 1996)

What! Cried Granny: An Almost Bedtime Story by Kate Lum (Puffin Books, 2002)

What Makes a Bird a Bird? by May Garelick (Mondo Publishing, 1995)

What Will the Weather Be? by Lynda DeWitt (HarperTrophy, 1993)

When Sophie Gets Angry—Really, Really Angry . . . by Molly Bang (Scholastic Paperbacks, 2004)

Widget by Lyn Rossiter McFarland (Farrar, Straus and Giroux, 2006)

Wings: A Tale of Two Chickens by James Marshall (Houghton Mifflin Company, 2003)

Wolf by Becky Bloom (Scholastic, Inc., 1999)

The Wolf's Story by Brenda Parkes (Rigby, 2000)

Worry Wart Wes by Tolya L. Thompson (Savor Publishing House, 2002)

Wow! It's Great Being a Duck by Joan Rankin (Aladdin, 2001)

Zipping, Zapping, Zooming Bats by Ann Earle (HarperTrophy, 1995)

Professional References

Cunningham, P. M., Hall, D. P., and Cunningham, J. W. (2000) *Guided Reading the Four-Blocks® Way.* Greensboro, NC: Carson-Dellosa Publishing Company.

Cunningham, P. M., Moore, S. A., Cunningham, J. W., and Moore, D. W. (2004) *Reading and Writing in Elementary Classrooms: Research Based K-4 Instruction, 5th Ed.* Boston, MA: Allyn and Bacon.

Duffy, G. G. (2003) *Explaining Reading: A Resource for Teaching Concepts, Skills, and Strategies.* New York, NY: The Guilford Press.

Harris, T. L. and Hodges, R. E. (Eds.) (1995) *The Literacy Dictionary: The Vocabulary of Reading and Writing.* Newark, DE: International Reading Association.

Harvey, S., and Goudvis, A. (2000) *Strategies That Work: Teaching Comprehension to Enhance Understanding.* York, ME: Stenhouse Publishers.

Keene, E. O. and Zimmermann, S. (1997) *Mosaic of Thought: Teaching Comprehension in a Reader's Workshop.* Portsmouth, NH: Heinemann.

Pearson, P. D., Roehler, L. R., Dole, J. A., and Duffy, G. G. (1992). "Developing Expertise in Reading Comprehension." In J. Samuels and A. Farstrup (Eds.) *What Research Has to Say About Reading Instruction, 2nd Ed.* Newark, DE: International Reading Association.

★ ★ ★ ★ ★ **Planning Form for Connecting a Book to Strategies and Skills**

Book Title _____

Author _____

Publisher _____ Year _____

ISBN _____

Synopsis _____

_____

_____

_____

❑ Connecting
   ❑ Text to Self
   ❑ Text to Text
   ❑ Text to World
❑ Predicting/Anticipating
❑ Summarizing
❑ Concluding
❑ Imaging
❑ Inferring
❑ Evaluating
❑ Applying
❑ Story Structure (Characters, Setting, Plot, Resolution)
❑ Expository Structure
❑ Problem/Solution
❑ Sequencing
❑ Cause/Effect

❑ Main Idea/Details
❑ Compare/Contrast
❑ Author's Purpose
❑ Figurative Language
   ❑ Metaphor
   ❑ Simile
   ❑ Hyperbole
   ❑ Idiom
   ❑ Onomatopoeia
   ❑ Alliteration
   ❑ Personification
❑ Context Clues
❑ Point of View
❑ Character Analysis
❑ Picture Clues
❑ Theme (Implied, Stated)
❑ Other _____

Notes:

★ ★ ★ ★ CD-104192 ★ Using Children's Literature to Enhance Reading Instruction

Strategy/Skill/ Text Feature	Book Used	Standard	Date Used

Strategy/Skill/ Text Feature	Book Used	Standard	Date Used
Predicting	Stephanie's Ponytail	1.B.1a	8/28
Sequencing	I Ain't Gonna Paint No More	1.C.1d	8/30
Predicting	Suddenly!	1.C.1d	9/1
Summarizing	A Present for Mom	1.C.1d	9/4
Story Structure	Ira Sleeps Over	2.A.1a	9/7
Summarizing	Green Wilma	1.C.1d	9/12
Predicting	Too Many Pumpkins	1.B.1a	9/15
Concluding	My Teacher Sleeps in School	2.B.2a	9/21
Concluding	Widget	2.B.2a	9/25
Inferring	A Present for Mom	1.B.1c	9/28
Summarizing	Giraffes Can't Dance	1.C.1d	10/3
Inferring	Give Maggie a Chance	1.B.1c	10/9

	A. Lincoln and Me	Agatha's Feather Bed	Alexander, Who Used to Be Rich Last Sunday	Annie and the Old One	Annie and the Wild Animals	Arnie the Doughnut	A Bad Case of Stripes	Baloney (Henry P.)	Because a Little Bug Went Ka-Choo!	Because Brian Hugged His Mother	Bedhead	Biggest, Strongest, Fastest	Book! Book! Book!	Boundless Grace	Bubble Gum, Bubble Gum	Chester the Out-of-Work Dog	Chickens Aren't the Only Ones
Theme	✓	✓		✓			✓								✓		
Picture Clues				✓	✓		✓							✓			
Character Analysis		✓															
Point of View							✓										
Context Clues				✓			✓										
Alliteration																	
Onomatopoeia											✓				✓		
Hyperbole	✓	✓									✓						
Idiom		✓															
Personification											✓						
Metaphor														✓			
Simile	✓	✓															
Author's Purpose												✓				✓	✓
Compare/Contrast	✓											✓		✓			✓
Main Idea/Details	✓		✓									✓					✓
Cause/Effect							✓		✓	✓						✓	✓
Sequencing					✓	✓							✓		✓		
Problem/Solution		✓				✓	✓					✓		✓		✓	
Expository Structure												✓					
Story Structure		✓	✓									✓				✓	
Applying										✓						✓	
Evaluating																	
Inferring																	
Imaging				✓													
Concluding				✓													
Summarizing			✓		✓						✓		✓			✓	
Predicting/Anticipating					✓				✓						✓		
Text to World		✓										✓		✓			
Text to Text			✓									✓		✓			
Text to Self							✓							✓			

Quick Reference to Books

Skill	Dandelions	Don't Need Friends	Dory Story	The Easter Egg Farm	First Day Jitters	Gasp!	The Giant Hug	Giggle, Giggle, Quack	Giraffes Can't Dance	Give Maggie a Chance	Grandpa's Teeth	Green Wilma	Hey, Mama Goose	The Honest-to-Goodness Truth	Hooway for Wodney Wat	Hottest, Coldest, Highest, Deepest	A House for Hermit Crab	How Is a Moose Like a Goose?
Theme	✓		✓							✓			✓	✓			✓	
Picture Clues					✓		✓					✓	✓					
Character Analysis	✓																	
Point of View																		
Context Clues			✓															
Alliteration																		
Onomatopoeia																		
Hyperbole	✓													✓				
Idiom																		
Personification										✓								
Metaphor																		
Simile	✓									✓			✓	✓				
Author's Purpose			✓													✓	✓	✓
Compare/Contrast												✓				✓		✓
Main Idea/Details																✓		✓
Cause/Effect						✓	✓					✓		✓	✓		✓	
Sequencing				✓			✓						✓				✓	
Problem/Solution			✓						✓	✓	✓		✓					
Expository Structure																✓	✓	✓
Story Structure		✓	✓	✓			✓				✓		✓	✓				
Applying		✓	✓						✓	✓			✓					
Evaluating																		
Inferring	✓	✓								✓								
Imaging										✓								
Concluding					✓		✓											
Summarizing		✓	✓	✓	✓		✓	✓			✓	✓	✓	✓				
Predicting/Anticipating		✓	✓		✓						✓							
Text to World		✓														✓	✓	✓
Text to Text						✓		✓	✓	✓			✓			✓		
Text to Self		✓			✓		✓			✓	✓		✓		✓		✓	

CD-104192 ★ Using Children's Literature to Enhance Reading Instruction

Quick Reference to Books

Skill	How Will We Get to the Beach?	I Ain't Gonna Paint No More	I Wanna Iguana	I Went Walking	Ira Sleeps Over	Is It Larger? Is It Smaller?	It Wasn't My Fault	Just Like You and Me	Just One More Story	Liar, Liar Pants on Fire	The Listening Walk	The Little Scarecrow Boy	A Log's Life	Loki and Alex	Mama, If You Had a Wish	Mike and the Bike	Missing: One Stuffed Rabbit	More Parts	More True Lies
Theme										✓				✓	✓		✓		
Picture Clues	✓			✓		✓				✓									
Character Analysis	✓																		
Point of View			✓												✓				
Context Clues																			
Alliteration								✓											
Onomatopoeia											✓								
Hyperbole																			
Idiom																		✓	
Personification																			
Metaphor																			
Simile								✓			✓								
Author's Purpose													✓	✓					
Compare/Contrast						✓			✓										
Main Idea/Details								✓					✓						
Cause/Effect	✓						✓						✓						
Sequencing	✓	✓			✓														
Problem/Solution	✓				✓												✓		
Expository Structure								✓											
Story Structure		✓			✓		✓		✓	✓		✓					✓		
Applying												✓				✓	✓		
Evaluating																			
Inferring												✓							
Imaging																			
Concluding																			✓
Summarizing		✓			✓					✓		✓			✓		✓		
Predicting/Anticipating	✓	✓		✓			✓					✓			✓				
Text to World			✓	✓							✓					✓	✓		✓
Text to Text			✓	✓					✓	✓							✓		
Text to Self			✓		✓		✓				✓				✓	✓	✓		

Quick Reference to Books

Skill	My Great-Aunt Arizona	My Teacher Sleeps in School	Never, EVER Shout in the Zoo	Night Noises	Night Tree	Once There Was a Bull . . . (frog)	Oops!	Ordinary Mary's Extraordinary Deed	Our Granny	The Pain and the Great One	The Paperboy	A Present for Mom	A Quiet Place	Salmon Creek	Smiley Shark	Something Beautiful	Souperchicken	Spiders Are Not Insects
Theme	✓										✓		✓			✓	✓	
Picture Clues			✓	✓		✓						✓						
Character Analysis	✓										✓					✓		
Point of View							✓			✓			✓					
Context Clues													✓					
Alliteration																		
Onomatopoeia			✓									✓						
Hyperbole																		
Idiom																	✓	
Personification				✓								✓	✓					
Metaphor																		
Simile				✓								✓	✓		✓			
Author's Purpose													✓					✓
Compare/Contrast	✓									✓								✓
Main Idea/Details									✓									✓
Cause/Effect			✓						✓								✓	
Sequencing				✓							✓	✓	✓					
Problem/Solution						✓						✓			✓		✓	
Expository Structure													✓					✓
Story Structure												✓			✓	✓	✓	
Applying								✓			✓		✓		✓			✓
Evaluating												✓	✓					✓
Inferring				✓	✓						✓							
Imaging	✓	✓			✓						✓		✓	✓				
Concluding		✓														✓		
Summarizing	✓					✓	✓			✓	✓	✓			✓	✓	✓	
Predicting/Anticipating			✓	✓	✓	✓						✓		✓				
Text to World									✓					✓	✓			
Text to Text			✓					✓	✓									
Text to Self	✓	✓			✓			✓	✓	✓		✓						

CD-104192 Using Children's Literature to Enhance Reading Instruction

Quick Reference to Books

Skill	Stand Tall, Molly Lou Melon	Stellaluna	Stephanie's Ponytail	The Stray Dog	Suddenly!	Swimmy	That's Good! That's Bad!	This Is the Way We Go to School	Today Was a Terrible Day	Tomorrow's Alphabet	Too Many Pumpkins	A Tree Is Nice	Unlovable	The Velveteen Rabbit	The Wednesday Surprise	Wemberly Worried	What Color Is Camouflage?	What! Cried Granny	What Makes a Bird a Bird?
Theme			✓			✓						✓					✓		
Picture Clues				✓	✓												✓		
Character Analysis	✓		✓														✓		
Point of View															✓				
Context Clues																			✓
Alliteration																			
Onomatopoeia	✓						✓												
Hyperbole	✓															✓			
Idiom																			
Personification																			
Metaphor												✓							
Simile	✓	✓	✓			✓	✓									✓			
Author's Purpose																	✓	✓	✓
Compare/Contrast		✓						✓											
Main Idea/Details												✓					✓		✓
Cause/Effect			✓	✓						✓				✓	✓		✓	✓	
Sequencing		✓	✓			✓				✓	✓							✓	
Problem/Solution				✓		✓					✓			✓	✓				
Expository Structure																	✓		
Story Structure	✓		✓	✓		✓				✓				✓	✓	✓	✓		
Applying	✓		✓						✓								✓		
Evaluating																			
Inferring														✓	✓	✓			
Imaging																			
Concluding					✓					✓					✓				
Summarizing	✓	✓		✓		✓				✓		✓		✓	✓	✓	✓		
Predicting/Anticipating			✓	✓	✓	✓	✓			✓	✓	✓			✓	✓			
Text to World			✓					✓											
Text to Text		✓					✓			✓	✓				✓		✓		
Text to Self	✓	✓		✓					✓	✓		✓		✓	✓	✓			

	What Will the Weather Be?	When Sophie Gets Angry—Really, Really Angry . . .	Widget	Wings: a Tale of Two Chickens	Wolf	The Wolf's Story	Wow! It's Great Being a Duck	Zipping, Zapping, Zooming Bats
Theme		✓		✓	✓			
Picture Clues			✓				✓	
Character Analysis				✓	✓			
Point of View						✓		
Context Clues			✓				✓	
Alliteration								
Onomatopoeia								
Hyperbole		✓						
Idiom								
Personification								
Metaphor								
Simile								
Author's Purpose	✓							✓
Compare/Contrast			✓					
Main Idea/Details	✓							✓
Cause/Effect	✓							
Sequencing					✓		✓	
Problem/Solution			✓				✓	
Expository Structure	✓							✓
Story Structure			✓		✓		✓	
Applying	✓	✓						
Evaluating	✓	✓						
Inferring			✓	✓	✓			
Imaging								
Concluding			✓					
Summarizing			✓	✓	✓	✓	✓	
Predicting/Anticipating							✓	
Text to World		✓				✓		✓
Text to Text								✓
Text to Self		✓						✓

★ ★ ★ ★ CD-104192 ★ **Using Children's Literature to Enhance Reading Instruction**